# The End of Mandatory Retirement: Effects on Higher Education

Karen C. Holden, *Editor*
University of Wisconsin, Madison

W. Lee Hansen, *Editor*
University of Wisconsin, Madison

**NEW DIRECTIONS FOR HIGHER EDUCATION**
MARTIN KRAMER, *Editor-in-Chief*
University of California, Berkeley

Number 65, Spring 1989

Paperback sourcebooks in
The Jossey-Bass Higher Education Series

Jossey-Bass Inc., Publishers
San Francisco • London

Karen C. Holden, W. Lee Hansen (eds.).
*The End of Mandatory Retirement: Effects on Higher Education.*
New Directions for Higher Education, no. 65.
Volume XVII, number 1.
San Francisco: Jossey-Bass, 1989.

**New Directions for Higher Education**
Martin Kramer, *Editor-in-Chief*

Copyright © 1989 by Jossey-Bass Inc., Publishers
and
Jossey-Bass Limited

Copyright under International, Pan American, and Universal Copyright Conventions. All rights reserved. No part of this issue may be reproduced in any form—except for brief quotation (not to exceed 500 words) in a review or professional work—without permission in writing from the publishers.

**New Directions for Higher Education** is published quarterly by Jossey-Bass Inc., Publishers (publication number USPS 990-880). *New Directions* is numbered sequentially—please order extra copies by sequential number. The volume and issue numbers above are included for the convenience of libraries. Second-class postage paid at San Francisco, California, and at additional mailing offices. POSTMASTER: Send address changes to Jossey-Bass Inc., Publishers, 350 Sansome Street, San Francisco, California 94104.

**Editorial correspondence** should be sent to the Editor-in-Chief, Martin Kramer, 2807 Shasta Road, Berkeley, California 94708.

Library of Congress Catalog Card Number LC 85-644752

International Standard Serial Number ISSN 0271-0560

International Standard Book Number ISBN 1-55542-866-5

Cover art by WILLI BAUM

Manufactured in the United States of America. Printed on acid-free paper.

# Ordering Information

The paperback sourcebooks listed below are published quarterly and can be ordered either by subscription or single copy.

Subscriptions cost $52.00 per year for institutions, agencies, and libraries. Individuals can subscribe at the special rate of $39.00 per year *if payment is by personal check*. (Note that the full rate of $52.00 applies if payment is by institutional check, even if the subscription is designated for an individual.) Standing orders are accepted.

Single copies are available at $12.95 when payment accompanies order. (California, New Jersey, New York, and Washington, D.C., residents please include appropriate sales tax.) For billed orders, cost per copy is $12.95 plus postage and handling.

Substantial discounts are offered to organizations and individuals wishing to purchase bulk quantities of Jossey-Bass sourcebooks. Please inquire.

Please note that these prices are for the calendar year 1989 and are subject to change without notice. Also, some titles may be out of print and therefore not available for sale.

To ensure correct and prompt delivery, all orders must give either the *name of an individual* or an *official purchase order number*. Please submit your order as follows:

*Subscriptions:* specify series and year subscription is to begin.
*Single Copies:* specify sourcebook code (such as, HE1) and first two words of title.

Mail orders for United States and Possessions, Latin America, Canada, Japan, Australia, and New Zealand to:
Jossey-Bass Inc., Publishers
350 Sansome Street
San Francisco, California 94104

Mail orders for all other parts of the world to:
Jossey-Bass Limited
28 Banner Street
London EC1Y 8QE

## New Directions for Higher Education Series
Martin Kramer, *Editor-in-Chief*

HE1 *Facilitating Faculty Development,* Mervin Freedman
HE2 *Strategies for Budgeting,* George Kaludis
HE3 *Services for Students,* Joseph Katz

HE4 *Evaluating Learning and Teaching,* C. Robert Pace
HE5 *Encountering the Unionized University,* Jack H. Schuster
HE6 *Implementing Field Experience Education,* John Duley
HE7 *Avoiding Conflict in Faculty Personnel Practices,* Richard Peairs
HE8 *Improving Statewide Planning,* James L. Wattenbarger, Louis W. Bender
HE9 *Planning the Future of the Undergraduate College,* Donald G. Trites
HE10 *Individualizing Education by Learning Contracts,* Neal R. Berte
HE11 *Meeting Women's New Educational Needs,* Clare Rose
HE12 *Strategies for Significant Survival,* Clifford T. Stewart, Thomas R. Harvey
HE13 *Promoting Consumer Protection for Students,* Joan S. Stark
HE14 *Expanding Recurrent and Nonformal Education,* David Harman
HE15 *A Comprehensive Approach to Institutional Development,* William Bergquist, William Shoemaker
HE16 *Improving Educational Outcomes,* Oscar Lenning
HE17 *Renewing and Evaluating Teaching,* John A. Centra
HE18 *Redefining Service, Research, and Teaching,* Warren Bryan Martin
HE19 *Managing Turbulence and Change,* John D. Millett
HE20 *Increasing Basic Skills by Developmental Studies,* John E. Roueche
HE21 *Marketing Higher Education,* David W. Barton, Jr.
HE22 *Developing and Evaluating Administrative Leadership,* Charles F. Fisher
HE23 *Admitting and Assisting Students After Bakke,* Alexander W. Astin, Bruce Fuller, Kenneth C. Green
HE24 *Institutional Renewal Through the Improvement of Teaching,* Jerry G. Gaff
HE25 *Assuring Access for the Handicapped,* Martha Ross Redden
HE26 *Assessing Financial Health,* Carol Frances, Sharon L. Coldren
HE27 *Building Bridges to the Public,* Louis T. Benezet, Frances W. Magnusson
HE28 *Preparing for the New Decade,* Larry W. Jones, Franz A. Nowotny
HE29 *Educating Learners of All Ages,* Elinor Greenberg, Kathleen M. O'Donnell, William Bergquist
HE30 *Managing Facilities More Effectively,* Harvey H. Kaiser
HE31 *Rethinking College Responsibilities for Values,* Mary Louise McBee
HE32 *Resolving Conflict in Higher Education,* Jane E. McCarthy
HE33 *Professional Ethics in University Administration,* Ronald H. Stein, M. Carlota Baca
HE34 *New Approaches to Energy Conservation,* Sidney G. Tickton
HE35 *Management Science Applications to Academic Administration,* James A. Wilson
HE36 *Academic Leaders as Managers,* Robert H. Atwell, Madeleine F. Green
HE37 *Designing Academic Program Reviews,* Richard F. Wilson
HE38 *Successful Responses to Financial Difficulties,* Carol Frances
HE39 *Priorities for Academic Libraries,* Thomas J. Galvin, Beverly P. Lynch
HE40 *Meeting Student Aid Needs in a Period of Retrenchment,* Martin Kramer
HE41 *Issues in Faculty Personnel Policies,* Jon W. Fuller
HE42 *Management Techniques for Small and Specialized Institutions,* Andrew J. Falender, John C. Merson
HE43 *Meeting the New Demand for Standards,* Jonathan R. Warren
HE44 *The Expanding Role of Telecommunications in Higher Education,* Pamela J. Tate, Marilyn Kressel
HE45 *Women in Higher Education Administration,* Adrian Tinsley, Cynthia Secor, Sheila Kaplan

HE46 *Keeping Graduate Programs Responsive to National Needs,*
Michael J. Pelczar, Jr., Lewis C. Solomon
HE47 *Leadership Roles of Chief Academic Officers,* David G. Brown
HE48 *Financial Incentives for Academic Quality,* John Folger
HE49 *Leadership and Institutional Renewal,* Ralph M. Davis
HE50 *Applying Corporate Management Strategies,* Roger J. Flecher
HE51 *Incentive for Faculty Vitality,* Roger G. Baldwin
HE52 *Making the Budget Process Work,* David J. Berg, Gerald M. Skogley
HE53 *Managing College Enrollments,* Don Hossler
HE54 *Institutional Revival: Case Histories,* Douglas W. Steeples
HE55 *Crisis Management in Higher Education,* Hal Hoverland, Pat McInturff, C. E. Tapie Rohm, Jr.
HE56 *Managing Programs for Learning Outside the Classroom,* Patricia Senn Breivik
HE57 *Creating Career Programs in a Liberal Arts Context,* Mary Ann F. Rehnke
HE58 *Financing Higher Education: Strategies After Tax Reform,* Richard E. Anderson, Joel W. Meyerson
HE59 *Student Outcomes Assessment: What Institutions Stand to Gain,* Diane F. Halpern
HE60 *Increasing Retention: Academic and Student Affairs Administrators in Partnership,* Martha McGinty Stodt, William M. Klepper
HE61 *Leaders on Leadership: The College Presidency,* James L. Fisher, Martha W. Tack
HE62 *Making Computers Work for Administrators,* Kenneth C. Green, Steven W. Gilbert
HE63 *Research Administration and Technology Transfer,* James T. Kenny
HE64 *Successful Strategic Planning: Case Studies,* Douglas W. Steeples

# Contents

*Editors' Notes* 1
Karen C. Holden, W. Lee Hansen

1. **Tax Changes, Retirement, and Pensions** 7
Alfred D. Sumberg

   The 1986 amendments to the ADEA and tax reforms from that year will require changes in retirement policies in higher education.

2. **Uncapping Mandatory Retirement:** 15
**The Lobbyists' Influence**
Henry J. Pratt

   Political, social, and legislative forces outside higher education orchestrated and directed congressional action to uncap the mandatory retirement age, paying little attention to the special nature of higher education.

3. **Retirement Behavior and Mandatory Retirement** 33
**in Higher Education**
Karen C. Holden, W. Lee Hansen

   Raising the mandatory retirement age from sixty-five to seventy is estimated to have relatively small, short-term effects on the retirement timing of tenured faculty members.

4. **Findings from the COFHE Studies** 51
Sarah Montgomery

   The results of the COFHE studies on the effects of raising the mandatory retirement age from sixty-five to seventy are presented.

5. **An Economywide View of Changing Mandatory** 63
**Retirement Rules**
Richard V. Burkhauser, Joseph F. Quinn

   Because of the strong disincentives to work that are embedded in social security and many employee pensions, most workers will continue to retire in their early sixties despite the uncapping of the mandatory retirement age.

6. **Eliminating Mandatory Retirement:** 73
**Effects on Retirement Age**
Karen C. Holden, W. Lee Hansen

   Uncapping the mandatory retirement age is unlikely to alter retirement age by much, but it will lead to substantially higher pensions for faculty members who continue to work.

7. **Implications of the 1986 ADEA Amendments for Tenure and Retirement** 85
*Oscar M. Ruebhausen*

Tenure arrangements are long-term contracts. If their duration is clear, they will protect academic freedom, provide institutions with the flexibility needed to meet changing circumstances, and comply with age-discrimination laws.

8. **Tenure After the ADEA Amendments: A Different View** 97
*Matthew W. Finkin*

To advocate the replacement of traditional tenure arrangements by fixed-term contracts is a misreading of the ADEA amendments. More important, it may threaten academic freedom.

*Index* 113

# Editors' Notes

The 1986 decision of Congress to eliminate the mandatory retirement age (MRA) has far-reaching implications for colleges, universities, and faculty. Traditionally, personnel policies, pension structures, and personal decisions about retirement have been tied to an explicit maximum age of retirement, defined by the MRA, but this is no longer true. Moreover, the speed with which Congress made the decision to uncap the MRA has left the educational community in transition and riddled by uncertainty. One can only speculate about the eventual impact that uncapping will have in these areas, but the need for guidance through the transition is apparent. The information presented in this sourcebook can help those who need to make more informed decisions about personnel, pensions, or retirement policies during this period.

The specific purpose of this volume is to inform the higher education community about the likely impacts—on faculty retirement patterns, retirement benefits, and academic tenure—of the 1986 federal legislation to uncap the MRA. Tenured faculty members are exempt from the uncapping provisions until January 1, 1994. Until that date, higher education will be examining what institutions can expect when uncapping does apply to tenured faculty members. The eight chapters in this volume discuss how uncapping and recent changes in the tax law alter the traditional structure of pensions, the meaning of normal retirement, and the implications for tenure. They present results from several previously unpublished studies, which examine how changes in the MRA influence faculty members' retirement decisions. Finally, they discuss potential changes in retirement patterns with an uncapped MRA, as well as the feasibility and legality of retirement policy changes in the new legal environment.

**Background**

For years, Representative Claude Pepper expressed his intention to eliminate mandatory retirement. Because several attempts to push for this change after 1978 (when the MRA was raised to seventy) had not succeeded, and because Congress had done little to investigate the effects of uncapping, a feeling prevailed in higher education that uncapping might never occur. The passage of the 1986 amendments to the Age Discrimination in Employment Act (ADEA), however, brought higher education face to face with the need to know more about several important retirement-related issues.

1. How would uncapping the MRA affect the average age of retirement?
2. If the average age of retirement rose, how would that affect the ability of colleges and universities to recruit new, younger faculty (particularly women and minorities)?
3. How would faculty members' salaries be affected as older, higher-paid faculty members continued teaching?
4. What could institutions do to encourage earlier retirement, and how much would such plans cost?
5. How might pension plans be restructured, to provide appropriate levels of replacement income during retirement without explicitly tying benefit levels to age?
6. How would uncapping affect the tenure system in higher education?

**Implications for Higher Education**

With the uncapping of the MRA, higher education faces many difficult decisions, because faculty members generally retire later than other workers. Moreover, defined contribution plans are much more prevalent in academe, and the pervasiveness of academic tenure reduces employers' flexibility with respect to personnel policies. Because of their shared concern for the welfare of higher education in general, a number of organizations—including the American Association of University Professors (AAUP), the Association of American Colleges, the National Association of College and University Business Officers, and others—have cooperated for decades to develop industrywide standards for retirement policies, pension systems, and the protection of academic freedom. The same organizations have taken the lead in examining the implications of uncapping for existing retirement policies. The AAUP (1987), for example, has already issued a report on the likely impact of uncapping and has concluded that there is little cause for alarm, but the report also notes that "the undeveloped state of research and knowledge regarding probable retirement behavior . . . is a deficiency that approaches scandal" (p. 17). (The AAUP group that prepared this report had access to some of the previously unpublished studies included in this volume.)

Because so little information is available to guide higher education in making the difficult but necessary decisions related to uncapping, it seems appropriate to collect in one sourcebook what we already know about the effects of lifting the MRA in academe. This information must be readily accessible to all members of the academic community as they seek to understand the full consequences of uncapping. Even with this volume, however, our knowledge about uncapping's impact on college and university administrations and on faculty members remains depressingly inadequate.

The first chapter, by Alfred D. Sumberg, summarizes the interrelated effects of recent legislation on faculty members' retirement behavior. In almost every year of the past decade, Congress passed legislation requiring changes in pension structures, taxes, or social security benefits. Sumberg focuses on the most recent of these changes: the 1983 amendments to the Social Security Act, the 1986 changes in the tax law, and the 1986 ADEA amendments. Understanding the meaning of these changes is difficult, not only because of their complexity but also because of delays in issuing their accompanying regulations and interpretations of those regulations.

In the second chapter, Henry J. Pratt traces the emergence of MRA policy in academe, as well as the political forces behind legislative initiatives to remove mandatory retirement practices. He then analyzes the nature of the strange and erratic struggle by higher education to forestall any change in mandatory retirement age for tenured faculty members. Pratt claims that higher education organized its opposition too late, failed to speak with a single voice, and was thoroughly outsmarted by members of Congress, who first favored raising the age of mandatory retirement to seventy and then favored uncapping the mandatory retirement age. Congressman Pepper's argument—that uncapping is a civil rights issue—dominated the arguments advanced by higher education: that uncapping would be more costly and complicated for higher education, that timing of the legislation was poor in light of current and prospective age distributions of faculty members, that faculty members and institutions could collaborate on a sensible retirement policy, and that this collaboration would improve the final result for all concerned.

**Current Knowledge**

The next three chapters summarize our current knowledge about retirement patterns and their sensitivity to changes in the mandatory retirement age. Karen C. Holden and W. Lee Hansen, in Chapter Three, present key findings from a congressionally mandated 1981 report on the impact of raising the MRA from sixty-five to seventy. On the basis of surveys of faculty members and institutions, Holden and Hansen estimate that this change would raise the average age of retirement by slightly more than one year for tenured faculty at institutions that previously had a mandatory retirement age of sixty-five. They also illustrate the effects of this change on institutional costs and on rates of hiring new faculty members.

Sarah Montgomery, in Chapter Four, presents the results of a study by the Consortium on the Financing of Higher Education (COFHE), an organization of thirty-two private colleges and universities, that looked at the effect of raising the MRA to seventy on its member campuses. The major finding of this study is that more faculty members than in the past would be likely to delay retirement by an average of about two years. Faculty members indicated, however, that this delay could be mitigated by incentive programs for early retirement.

In Chapter Five, Richard V. Burkhauser and Joseph F. Quinn present findings from their study of retirement behavior in the entire U.S. work force. They conclude that raising the MRA will not appreciably affect older workers, primarily because so many of them already retire well before age sixty-five. At the same time, Burkhauser and Quinn admit that higher education is different enough to feel more substantial effects from a raised MRA and from uncapping.

How can we help people and institutions adapt to a world where nobody can be required to retire on the basis of age alone? In Chapter Six, Karen C. Holden and W. Lee Hansen explore how the lifting of this particular anchor affects the setting of retirement benefits.

**Implications for Tenure**

The final two chapters explore the effects of uncapping on tenure. Chapter Seven, by Oscar M. Ruebhausen, presents the view that fixed-term contracts of some kind must be devised to deal with uncapping. Ruebhausen argues that tenure appointments will now make it extremely difficult to retire older faculty members whose productivity and performance are waning.

In Chapter Eight, Matthew W. Finkin takes issue with Ruebhausen. Finkin argues that fixed-term contracts are of doubtful validity, not only under the ADEA but also under the AAUP's 1940 statement of principles. On balance, he argues, the costs of living with uncapping are less than those of any alternative, and abandonment of tenure would be "a dangerous overreaction" to uncapping.

**Conclusion**

This sourcebook represents an attempt to inform the higher education community about the potential consequences of uncapping. Considerable alarm has been expressed by some institutions, and radical changes have been proposed for pensions and tenure. It would be unfortunate if such changes were made without careful thought and evidence for their need and effectiveness. In fact, higher education has failed to mobilize its resources to examine and monitor the impact of retirement-related legislation. This is ironic in light of higher education's long-standing support for industrywide retirement standards. Institutions should have been particularly mindful of legislation having important long- and short-term consequences.

Until additional evidence is assembled, we must rely on whatever information is available to help faculty members and their institutions during the transition to complete uncapping, which will take effect in 1994. The information presented here is designed to facilitate that process.

The research for Chapter 3 and Chapter 6 was supported in part by a contract (J-9-E-9-0067) from the Department of Labor. Additional support for computer work was provided by the Center for Demography and Ecology at the University of Wisconsin-Madison, supported in part by National Institute of Child Health and Human Development Grant HD 05876. The views expressed here do not necessarily reflect those of the funding sources. We have been assisted periodically by several research assistants, including Paul Boldin, Robin Stonecash, and Brian Rittenhouse. We thank the Survey Research Center at the University of Wisconsin for their expert assistance in developing and conducting the surveys.

We are grateful for the support of the Lilly Endowment for a conference at which several of the chapters in this volume were presented as papers. In helping us bring that collection of papers to publishable form, we gratefully acknowledge the editorial assistance of Beverly Schrag and, of course, the authors who patiently wrote and rewrote their chapters in response to unexpected legislative changes. We thank Martin Kramer, editor-in-chief of this series, for his encouragement in bringing this manuscript to publication.

Karen C. Holden<br>
W. Lee Hansen<br>
Editors

**Reference**

American Association of University Professors. "Working Paper on the Status of Tenure Without Mandatory Retirement." *Academe,* 1987, *73* (3), 5-18.

*Karen C. Holden is senior scientist, Institute for Research on Poverty and the Institute of Aging, University of Wisconsin-Madison.*

*W. Lee Hansen is professor of economics and of education policy studies, University of Wisconsin-Madison.*

*The 1986 amendments to the ADEA and tax reforms from that year will require changes in retirement policies in higher education.*

# Tax Changes, Retirement, and Pensions

*Alfred D. Sumberg*

The early 1980s found policymakers searching for responses to several economic changes, a search that over the next few years would result in legislation altering the fundamental structure of retirement policies in higher education. Perhaps most significant among these changes was the economic consequence of a "graying" population, a distributional change driven by smaller cohorts of young adults and continuing increases in life expectancy for older adults. For the social security system, this meant projections of short-term and long-term deficits. Short-term deficits were predicted from the combination of high inflation and high unemployment in the late 1970s; long-term deficits would result from the population's aging. Meanwhile, the economy battled with large deficits in the domestic budget and with the effects of moving from creditor to debtor status in international trade. Against this backdrop, federal officials called for educational reforms at all levels, including colleges and universities, to improve the quality of curricula and the abilities of graduates.

Two failures and a congressional election served as the background of retirement-policy initiatives between 1983 and 1986, which attempted to remedy these economic conditions. The Reagan administration failed in 1981 to implement its plan to reduce social security benefits through a combination of benefit and age-eligibility changes. In 1982, Representative Claude Pepper, chair of the House Select Committee on Aging, led an equally unsuccessful fight to amend the Age Discrimination in Employment Act (ADEA) to eliminate mandatory retirement. (The congressional election of 1982 hinged partly on the question of which party was more committed to protecting social security benefits, a debate that the Republicans lost as the voters returned an even stronger Democratic majority to the House.) Yet both of these initially doomed attempts were ultimately successful. Tax legislation enacted in 1985 and 1986 also touched on important pension issues.

**Social Security Amendments of 1983**

The Social Security Amendments of 1983 (P.L. 98-21) pointed the direction that Congress and the Reagan administration would take over the next three years in changing retirement policy. Tax and income policies would aim primarily at encouraging later retirement.

National distress over an impending deficit in the trust fund of the Old Age and Survivors Insurance served as the catalyst for the National Commission on Social Security Reform, created by executive order in December 1981. Its recommendations, reported to the president early in 1983, resolved the short-run deficit and a portion of the long-run deficit by raising tax rates. It remained for Congress to eliminate the long-run deficit entirely, which it did (with little dissent) by raising the age at which unreduced social security benefits would be paid. In the year 2000, that age will begin gradually to increase, reaching age sixty-six first for workers turning age sixty-two in 2005 and, finally, reaching age sixty-seven for those turning age sixty-two in 2022 or later. While benefits will still be paid at age sixty-two, eventually they will be reduced actuarially by 30 percent, rather than the current 20 percent. Although this incentive for early retirement has been reduced, the incentive for deferring social security payments beyond the age of eligibility for full benefits (now sixty-five) will be raised through a gradual increase in the delayed-retirement credit from 3 to 8 percent between 1995 and 2013.

In minor ways, other provisions of the 1983 social security amendments may change the future retirement income of faculty members in higher education. For example, mandatory coverage was extended to newly hired federal workers and to all employees of nonprofit organizations; no longer could state and local government employees vote to withdraw from the system. Thus, while public colleges and universities that were not already covered by social security in 1983 could remain outside the system, no covered institutions could withdraw. An offset provision for spouse beneficiaries who also receive pensions from noncovered work was modified so that retired workers' benefits also became subject to offset, beginning in 1986. This change was designed to ensure that certain people—who had substantial earnings and pensions from work not covered by social security—would not be treated as if they were low-income workers. And, finally, for the first time ever, social security benefits became taxable, with half of any benefits received now counted as taxable income for higher-income beneficiaries.

Immediately after the 1984 election, concern shifted from social security deficits to tax reform and deficits in the consolidated budget. Representative Pepper's failure to eliminate mandatory retirement in 1982 also left a sensitive political issue on the national agenda. This led him to introduce legislation that would amend the Age Discrimination in Employment Act of 1967. Little did Pepper realize how inextricably linked by circumstances was his legislation to the tax debates in 1985 and 1986. While the higher education community finally roused itself to testify on the Pepper amendments, it failed to initially realize that tax reform would have an equally important impact on retirement policy and on the ability of colleges and universities to respond, through changes in pension structure, to the income needs and changing demographic makeup of their employees.

### Mandatory Retirement Age and Tax Changes

Four pieces of legislation passed in 1985 and 1986 made significant changes in coverage rules and in the nature of pensions and retirement policies in higher education. The first, the Consolidated Omnibus Budget Reconciliation Act (COBRA) of 1985 (P.L. 99-272), a law that mandated changes in government programs in order to meet deficit reduction goals, extended the provisions of the ADEA (and its 1978 amendments) to the health policies of employers, who were now required to provide comparable benefits to all workers between the ages of forty and seventy under a group health plan. No longer could medical benefits be reduced at age sixty-five, when Medicare was made available to eligible workers; Medicare now became a secondary payer, after nondiscriminatory employer-sponsored plans.

While COBRA appeared to have only a minor effect on benefit plans in higher education, the 1986 amendments to ADEA did much more. They prohibited mandatory retirement at any age for all workers except—until January 1, 1994—police officers, firefighters, and tenured faculty members. On the same day that the House and the Senate gave final approval to the ADEA amendments, the House approved the conference report on the Omnibus Budget Reconciliation Act (OBRA) of 1986 (P.L. 99-509), which pondered yet another change. OBRA amended the Employee Retirement Income Security Act, the Internal Revenue Code (IRC), and the ADEA such that, after December 31, 1987, pension plans could not reduce or stop benefit accruals or continued contributions to an employee's pension account after some fixed age. (It is legal, however, for defined-benefit plans to set limits on maximum years of service.) In addition, OBRA prohibited employers from denying pension coverage to employees hired within five years of a plan's normal retirement age, (although employers could establish a "floating" normal retirement age for these employees, which could not be later than five years after initial participation).

What was the significance for higher education of these three measures? For all higher education employees except tenured faculty members, mandatory retirement was immediately prohibited, and age limits on continued pension accruals were voided. The importance of the OBRA legislation, which applied ADEA age limits to participation in employer-sponsored group health plans, also became apparent: The removal of the age limit now required that health insurance coverage be extended to employees who were seventy and older. ADEA temporarily allowed tenured faculty members to be retired as early as age seventy (provided that states or institutions had not prohibited mandatory retirement), but faculty members could continue under OBRA to participate in employer-sponsored health insurance plans, and under COBRA to have pension benefits accrue beyond the age of seventy. Unless additional legislation mandates otherwise, the latter privilege will be extended to all faculty members on January 1, 1994.

The higher education community discussed ways to develop retirement incentives that would discourage faculty members from continuing full-time employment beyond age seventy (after the MRA is uncapped). At the same time, the Tax Reform Act (TRA) of 1986 reduced the considerable autonomy and flexibility that higher education institutions and other nonprofit organizations had enjoyed in administering their pension accounts. Four goals of Congress are apparent in that legislation:

- To slow the rapid growth of pensions (and thus the revenue loss) that had been fueled by the special tax treatment provided to pensions under the IRC of 1954
- To ensure that contributions to all tax-sheltered pension plans, including so-called 403(b) plans (named after their IRC number), were used solely for retirement pensions, rather than for sheltered savings accumulated for other reasons or as bequests to survivors
- To extend the nondiscriminatory provisions required of qualified pension plans under the IRC to all tax-deferred retirement savings, such that the design of pension plans (through coverage, benefits, and financing) could not favor highly compensated employees
- To discourage the use of tax-deferred arrangements as early-retirement incentives.

To accomplish the first goal—slowing the growth of tax-deferred savings—TRA set strict limits on the amount of pretax income that could be contributed to the popular 403(b) plans, on the maximum benefits payable under defined-benefit plans, and on the maximum annual contribution to defined contribution plans. Defined-benefit plans may pay no more than $90,000 or 100 percent of the employee's average compensation during the three highest-earnings years (whichever amount is less). Defined-contribution plans may contribute no more than $30,000 or 25 percent of the employee's compensation (whichever is less). The defined-benefit limit will rise according to changes in the Consumer Price Index (CPI), but the defined-contribution limit will remain frozen until a 4:1 ratio in these limits is reached. The maximum contribution to section 403(b) plans made through salary reduction is set at $9,500 annually, but is later to rise with the CPI. (See Employee Benefit Research Institute, 1987, for information on provisions that apply to employees who are close to retirement.) In addition, tax-deferred contributions to individual retirement accounts (which, in fewer than five years, had accumulated $23 billion) could no longer be made by married individuals (filing jointly) with an adjusted gross income of more than $50,000 or by unmarried individuals with an income greater than $35,000 (exceptions are made for individuals not eligible to participate in employer-sponsored plans).

To ensure that funds could not be sheltered and then withdrawn for purposes other than retirement, TRA imposed immediate penalties for early and delayed withdrawal. Distribution of new contributions from qualified retirement plans, from section 403(b) and section 401(k) plans, and from individual retirement accounts before an individual reaches age fifty-nine and one-half now incurs a 10 percent tax penalty. This surtax can be avoided only under three conditions: if the distribution is made through an annuity payable over the expected lifetime of the individual, if the distribution is made after age fifty-five and total retirement, or if the distribution is used to pay medical expenses to the extent that they are deductible under federal tax laws. Effective after January 1, 1989, however, no early withdrawal before age fifty-nine and one-half is allowed in the case of 403(b) plans that involve salary-reduction agreements (except for separation from service and financial hardship; the early-distribution penalty does not apply to section 457 plans, which are commonly used by state and local governments). Finally, TRA changed the tax treatment of lump-sum distributions, phasing out their capital-gains treatment over six years and permitting a one-time election of five-year forward averaging after age fifty-nine and one-half (which eliminates the more advantageous ten-year forward averaging under prior tax law).

To prohibit individuals from preserving pensions as a form of life insurance for heirs, the TRA also required all pension plans after December 31, 1988, to provide for minimum distribution of benefits no later than the year following an employee's reaching age seventy and one-half. There is a 50 percent surtax on the difference between the amount actually distributed (even if that is zero) and the required minimum. That minimum is defined by the amount necessary to ensure full payout over the lifetime of the individual. Nevertheless, because this requirement presented a problem for government pensions, which under state and local laws cannot pay the full annuity amounts when an employee is simultaneously paid for continued work, Congress exempted employees from the surtax if they were eligible for state or local government pensions.

Since 1942, the IRC has required that "qualified" plans—those in which employers' pension contributions are considered tax-deductible business expenses—meet certain nondiscriminatory criteria. Educational institutions are nonprofit organizations, and so qualification of their plans was unnecessary. Thus, colleges and universities were allowed considerable flexibility in developing separate pension plans for faculty members and in offering special early-retirement benefits to them. For example, some institutions had portable defined-contribution plans for faculty members and nonportable defined-benefit plans for all other employees. Other institutions may have covered all employees under single plans but provided more generous benefits to faculty members, by making higher contribution rates for them or by using a more steeply graded integration with social security.

Unless new guidelines appear, the nondiscrimination requirements specified in the IRC (as amended in 1942) will apply from now on to all tax-sheltered annuities except those maintained by churches. These rules require that a pension plan not discriminate in favor of highly paid employees. Specifically, they require that a plan also cover a specified percentage of its lower-paid employees and that tax-deferred contributions be comparable across groups of covered employees. Under these rules, it may be necessary to give all employees the tax deferments that some plans now offer only to faculty members.

The exact effects of the TRA rules on coverage and benefits for faculty members will not be known until new regulations define highly compensated employees, on the one hand, and employee groups, on the other. In documents provided by the staff of the Joint Tax Committee to the House Ways and Means Committee, teachers were characterized as highly compensated employees. Therefore, pensions that cover only faculty members may have to be restructured before they can continue to qualify as tax-deferred annuities.

**Conclusion**

A major restructuring of pension plans in higher education may be required, particularly because of the TRA's extension of nondiscrimination rules to all tax-deferred annuities. Tax rules limiting contributions, specifying maximum benefits, and restricting early and delayed distributions from these plans may likewise restrict the ability of institutions to structure incentives for retirement that are targeted to particular employee, age, or salary groups.

The changes discussed in this chapter are unlikely to alter either retirement benefits or timing of retirement for faculty members who leave before 1990. Despite the growth in early retirement among the U.S. workforce in general, higher education's predominantly male faculty members will probably continue to retire later than average, but before age seventy. Perhaps as social security and tax rules discourage early retirement and allow employees to continue working, to retain their health insurance, and to accrue pension benefits beyond age seventy, attitudes toward retirement among a new generation of faculty members will change. Such new attitudes could lead even more faculty members to continue teaching and research beyond age seventy.

This analysis says nothing about the costs or benefits to colleges and universities of delayed retirement, but it seems clear that recent legislation will have a larger impact on pension design in higher education than its authors (and perhaps even the higher education community) contemplated. Any effort to improve and expand pension coverage for faculty members, through higher employer contributions or tax-deferred employee contributions, must operate within the new tax environment. The new rules also restrict the ability of employers to alter coverage and benefits in order to encourage early retirement by a single group of employees.

Over the next few years, the higher education community will have to accommodate itself to the uncapping of the mandatory retirement age, in a manner consistent with restrictions placed on pension and health policies. Such accommodation, it is hoped, will reflect the traditional resiliency of higher education in adapting to changes in the social and legal environment. At the same time, higher education will have an opportunity to offer innovative pension arrangements to its employees, including the great majority, who are not tenured faculty members.

**References**

Employee Benefit Research Institute. *Fundamentals of Employee Benefit Programs.* (3rd ed.) Washington, D.C.: Employee Benefit Research Institute, 1987.

*Alfred D. Sumberg is associate general secretary of the American Association of University Professors, Washington, D.C.*

*Political, social, and legislative forces outside higher education orchestrated and directed congressional action to uncap the mandatory retirement age, paying little attention to the special nature of higher education.*

# Uncapping Mandatory Retirement: The Lobbyists' Influence

*Henry J. Pratt*

Any attempt to understand congressional action on uncapping the MRA should take account of earlier congressional efforts on the same issue, for the forces at work in any policy area are likely to closely resemble those that have shaped policy in the past. In this chapter, I focus on the federal regulation of mandatory retirement practices, with special attention to higher education. I identify and analyze the longer-term political forces that underlay the struggles on Capitol Hill over mandatory retirement, first in 1977 and 1978 and then in 1985 and 1986.

In examining these struggles, I ask three key questions: Before 1977, why was higher education almost totally uninvolved in the anti-age-discrimination movement, even though educational institutions are large employers, and even though the movement had been active for many years? Why was the academic sector surprised by the 1977-78 legislation, which raised the legally permissible MRA from sixty-five to seventy? Why was the higher education lobby also unable to exert political influence a decade later, when legislation on total uncapping of the MRA was introduced?

## The 1967 ADEA

The campaign to achieve federal legislation on age discrimination in employment was launched by the 1961 White House Conference on Aging. The conference was organized by the Eisenhower administration, whose guiding political philosophy was incompatible with any far-reaching domestic policy initiatives. Nevertheless, the Section on Employment and Retirement affirmed (without recommending any legislation) the desirability of eliminating "discrimination in hiring based on age by means of federal, state, and local legislation and by voluntary programs," as well as the need for "steps to prevent mandatory, compulsory retirement at an arbitrarily designated age" (White House Conference on Aging, 1961, pp. 150-155).

In the next five years, age discrimination in employment became a fixed topic on the national agenda. Bills were introduced in Congress and debated in committees. A Department of Labor survey reported widespread discrimination against older workers (U.S. Department of Labor, 1965). President Lyndon B. Johnson issued an executive order prohibiting age discrimination by contractors and subcontractors paid from federal funds. In January 1967, President Johnson requested congressional action on age discrimination: "Hundreds of thousands not yet old . . . find themselves jobless because of age discrimination. In economic terms, this is a serious and senseless loss to a nation on the move. But the greater loss is the cruel sacrifice in happiness and well-being, which joblessness imposes on those citizens and their families" (Johnson, 1967, p. 37). The resulting bill—the 1967 Age Discrimination in Employment Act—initially covered only the private sector. While it protected workers between the ages of forty and sixty-five from age-related employment practices, it still permitted mandatory retirement below age sixty-five when this provision was part of a bona fide pension plan.

In one sense, the 1967 ADEA was a setback for those advocating the interests of elderly persons who were still able and willing to work, since it did not alter the prevalent practice of mandatory retirement at age sixty-five. Indeed, by refusing to protect workers beyond age sixty-four, Congress implicitly reaffirmed the long-standing industry practice of mandatory retirement at that age. Advocates for the elderly, however, could derive some hope from language in the bill that authorized the secretary of labor to recommend legislation that would change the protected age. The secretary of labor was also authorized to study practices that were conducive to involuntary retirement. As it happened, neither of these provisions produced any specific legislative change, yet they no doubt affected the general political atmosphere in a way compatible with later reform.

### Increased Focus on Mandatory Retirement

In the early 1970s, governmental and nongovernmental institutions alike began a sustained effort to extend ADEA protection to persons over sixty-five years of age. The American Association of Retired Persons (AARP), united at the national level with the National Retired Teachers Association (NRTA), was particularly active in this regard. Although AARP representatives testified in favor of the 1967 ADEA, they did so with reluctance, lest it appear that the organization was accepting the upper age limit contained in the bill.

The first significant victory in AARP's efforts occurred at the White House Conference on Aging in 1971. As the conference approached, AARP and NRTA published a book in which scholars and former governmental officials, including anthropologist Margaret Mead, economist Juanita Kreps, and former HEW secretary Wilbur Cohen, called for an end to mandatory retirement (Abrams and Robinson, 1971). At the conference itself, AARP fought for passage of a resolution declaring any MRA to be unconstitutional. Unwilling to endorse the AARP/NRTA position, the conference instead adopted a statement on the need for greater enforcement of existing federal, state, and local anti-age-discrimination laws. A subordinate clause of this "better enforcement" theme did suggest the need to eliminate the age limit of sixty-five in age-discrimination legislation, as well as a possible expansion of ADEA to cover all employees in the public and private sectors. Moreover, another resolution affirmed that "chronological age should not be the sole criterion for retirement. A flexible policy should be adopted . . . [and] employment opportunities after age sixty-five must be made available" (White House Conference on Aging, 1971, pp. 3-4). While this was not a ringing victory for the AARP/NRTA point of view, it was a significant step towards its goals.

The ADEA was amended in 1974 to cover employees of state and national governments, and the Age Discrimination Act of 1975 barred discrimination on the basis of age in all federally assisted programs and activities. The 1975 act directly affected 100,000 public and private entities (schools, hospitals, and so on) receiving federal assistance and as many as 450,000 subrecipients—that is, those receiving aid from directly aided institutions (Schuck, 1980). It did not prohibit mandatory retirement, however, which was permitted under a provision allowing age criteria to be employed where "established under authority of any law."

Soon other forces pressed for additional changes. One came in the form of court interpretations of the 1967 act. One of its sections allowed for continued observation of the terms of any bona fide seniority system or employee pension plan, a provision that some courts interpreted as allowing mandatory retirement of pension-covered workers before age sixty-five. Many congressmen believed that these court rulings were contrary to congressional intent and that the 1967 act needed a clarifying amendment.

Another change grew out of what some people saw (with only slight exaggeration) as impending bankruptcy in the social security system. This fiscal crisis, due primarily to high rates of inflation and unemployment in the late 1970s, led Congress in 1977 to reassess social security financing. The ultimate resolution was a massive increase in the payroll withholding tax, the biggest tax increase in peacetime U.S. history.

Some people, however, argued that raising the mandatory retirement age to allow able and willing employees to continue working beyond age sixty-five would alleviate social security's fiscal problems. This view was heard from various academic experts, including Juanita Kreps, soon to become the first secretary of commerce in the Carter administration. An article on the editorial page of the *New York Times* described the possible economic gains to social security of uncapping the MRA—if Congress would take one simple, bold step: "A saving of $2.25 billion a year is waiting to drop into the lap of the hard-pressed Social Security Trust system at no cost to the taxpayer. All that needs to be done is for Congress to act on a bill that has been kicking around the legislative hopper for years.... The bill ... would put an end to mandatory retirement at sixty-five" (Altman, 1977, p. 17).

**The Campaign Finds Leadership**

Weaving the various forces in favor of amending the Age Discrimination Act into a coherent pattern required a skilled congressional tactician. This person proved to be Representative Claude Pepper of Florida. Pepper's strong convictions on mandatory retirement dated back to 1974, when he was appointed to the newly created House Select Committee on Aging. Under its original chairman, Representative William Randall of New Jersey, the Committee on Aging had not been especially concerned with workers who were sixty-five and older. The committee remained in that posture until January 1977, when Randall stepped down and Pepper replaced him. A man still vigorous and alert in his middle seventies, with vast congressional experience, Pepper personified the cause he now sought to advance.

Within a month of becoming chairman, Pepper launched a series of hearings into MRA-related practices. During committee hearings in March 1977, Pepper encouraged witnesses who were friendly to his views and showed displeasure with those who disagreed. Pepper and his allies occasionally drew on performance and productivity measures to support greater employment opportunities for the elderly. These arguments, however, were clearly less persuasive than the argument that eliminating mandatory retirement was a moral issue. Some weeks after the hearings, the committee released its report, which attacked mandatory retirement and concluded with a point-by-point refutation of the case offered in defense of MRA-related practices (U.S. House of Representatives, 1977).

Pepper made strong efforts to persuade other members of the House to accept his viewpoint. He prodded the Equal Opportunities Subcommittee of the Education and Labor Committee, a body with jurisdiction over the bill, whose chairman was Representative Augustus C. Hawkins of California. It also appears that Pepper appealed for prompt action to the other House committees that had similar jurisdiction.

Representative Harrison Williams of New Jersey, chair of the Senate Special Committee on Aging and the Senate Human Resources Committee, avoided Pepper's flamboyant style. A strong advocate of uncapping the MRA, Williams guided the Senate version of Pepper's bill through the required committee hearings and later served as the bill's chief sponsor on the Senate floor. In addition to the leadership provided by key lawmakers in the House and the Senate, the AARP—with a longstanding interest in mandatory retirement, and with resources to mount a major lobbying effort (Ford, 1978-79)—played an important role.

Leaders in the campaign to forbid mandatory retirement at a designated age had succeeded in getting their concern placed firmly on the agenda of Congress. A long-existing sentiment that something ought to be done about perfecting the ADEA was now transformed into the conviction that the matter merited immediate consideration and possible action.

In 1977, H.R. 5383, an amalgam of bills previously submitted by Pepper and two other congressmen, was voted out by the House Subcommittee on Employment Opportunities. The subcommittee bill had three principal provisions: to eliminate fixed-age retirement for federal employees; to raise the upper age limit of ADEA protection from sixty-five to seventy for private, state, and local employees; and to close the pension loophole under which employees could be forced to retire before age sixty-five. Just five weeks later, a surprising announcement was made: The chairs of the two other committees with jurisdiction over retirement—the committee on Post Office and Civil Service and the Committee on Education and Labor—had agreed that no more hearings were needed. The following day, the House Rules Committee voted to clear the measure for a floor vote. The pace at which these developments moved through Congress was remarkable. So intense was the momentum that, had the summer recess not intervened, the House might have adopted the measure immediately.

## Higher Education Bestirs Itself

Only when the House was on the verge of a final vote, and when the Senate Labor Subcommittee was moving toward recommending favorable action by its parent committee, did Washington's lobbyists for higher education become aware of their stake in these developments. Thomas A. Bartlett, the newly installed head of the Association of American Universities (AAU), notified the executive heads of the AAU's member institutions of the pending legislation and enclosed a copy of a memorandum prepared several days earlier by the American Council on Education's (ACE) Office of Governmental Relations. Thus began a short-lived but frenetic period of lobbying.

Why did the higher education lobby wait until the eleventh hour to become active? There were two apparent reasons. First, the higher education community had not regarded the earlier anti-age-discrimination movement as a serious threat to its interests, since virtually no college or university had an MRA of under sixty-five. Second, the unprecedented speed of the 1977 legislative steamroller would have rendered it difficult to mount an effective defense of the status quo even if the nature of the threat had been correctly perceived.

Two additional factors bear mentioning. The first is that the several groups constituting Washington's higher education lobby were in disarray. For some years, the Association of American Colleges (AAC) had been viewed as a leader on national legislative issues related to higher education, by virtue of its long institutional history (it was founded in 1915), its high-prestige membership (including many old, distinguished four-year institutions), and its large size (more than six hundred members). In 1976, however, the AAC board announced that henceforth the group would devote its energies to promoting the substance of liberal education. To fill the gap, a new organization, the National Association of Independent Colleges and Universities (NAICU), sprang into existence. Although relations between AAC and NAICU were cordial, the general situation was, to say the least, unsettling. In the quest to articulate the views of colleges and universities on the MRA issue, leadership was assumed by still another organization, the AAU. Yet, with only a small and select membership—primarily large, research-oriented institutions—AAU was not in a position to speak as convincingly for higher education as a more inclusive body could ("Private Colleges Seek Balanced Student Aid," February 22, 1977, p. 10).

The second factor is that all colleges and universities did not have an equal stake in protecting an institution's right to force retirement of professors at some age before seventy. A joint 1950 statement by the American Association of University Professors (AAUP) and the AAC embraced mandatory retirement as a permissible ground for the termination of an academic appointment and stated that the appropriate age of mandatory retirement should be "between sixty-five and seventy inclusive" (American Association of University Professors, 1950, pp. 115-116). In accord with these recommendations, many institutions of higher education set the mandatory retirement age at sixty-five, while a substantial minority set the MRA at seventy (see Chapter Three in this volume). The nation's colleges and universities did not agree on the virtues of maintaining an MRA below seventy, and this disagreement may well have delayed their representatives' political intervention and diminished their forcefulness when they finally did speak up.

Nevertheless, under the leadership of AAU's Thomas A. Bartlett, the higher education lobby mounted an energetic campaign, one that was at least partly successful. AAU prodded the presidents of its member universities, as well as college and university presidents not formally affiliated with AAU, to write or call the Labor Subcommittee of the Senate Human Relations Committee. It also urged other higher education associations to get involved.

The leaders of this campaign gave several reasons for exempting professors from the MRA-related provisions of the proposed legislation. Without such exemption, they said, the number of job openings for able young people would be reduced as older faculty members continued to work. Affirmative action on behalf of women and minorities would also be stymied. Moreover, institutions would suffer additional financial pressure because of higher salaries for senior employees and additional retirement contributions. Congressional staffers were quick to point out that the same objections had been made, to no avail, by the business community.

Only two arguments that academia was different from other large employers had any influence on Congress. One was a predicted oversupply of tenured older professors, brought on by the "bulge" of faculty members hired during the expansion of the 1950s and the 1960s. The other was the difficulty of determining when a faculty member's performance had declined enough to justify terminating his or her employment "for cause" (academic tenure has never been construed as protecting an employee against dismissal when a basis for "cause" is identified and then proved). Lobbyists argued that if mandatory retirement were abolished or the upper age limit were raised, tenure would be threatened. Universities might have to conduct frequent evaluations of all their professors, at all ages. Such reviews might be costly, demoralizing, and inconclusive.

## Senate Action on the Chafee Amendment

In September 1977, Senator John Chafee of Rhode Island proposed amending the Senate bill in line with AAU demands. The amendment would permit colleges and universities to maintain compulsory retirement at a specified age, sixty-five or above, for faculty members who were "serving on a contract of unlimited tenure" or who had noncontractual arrangements that provided for tenure (U.S. Senate, 1977, p. 8). The Senate Committee on Human Resources voted to accept Chafee's proposal. The bill was reported out in that form by the committee and later came before the full Senate.

By the time the issue came up for debate on the Senate floor in mid October, however, opposition had developed. Senator Alan Cranston of California led the anti-Chafee forces. As had been true throughout the campaign to eliminate mandatory retirement, Cranston's opening remarks to oppose exempting professors were moral in tone, appealing to the principles of equal rights (U.S. Congress, 1977). Senator Chafee, speaking for the other side, employed arguments specific to higher education. He said that tenure, while it should not be abolished, nevertheless restricted employment opportunities for younger faculty members in an era of financial retrenchment, and he went on to develop a second theme: that objective evaluation of employees' performance may be feasible in other kinds of organizations, but the traditions of academe make such evaluation virtually impossible as a precursor to possible dismissal of tenured professors.

The remarkable thing about the Senate floor debate was that the only major point of controversy was the status of tenured professors under the bill. This issue had not been mentioned during the public hearings in either house. As a result, senators had no information on it. Since committee hearings, mail from constituents, and conversations with trusted lobbyists—the sources of information that lawmakers typically draw on to inform their thinking—played no role in this case, the senators had to rely more heavily on the substance of the floor debate than typically would have been the case. Although there is no way of knowing exactly how most senators made up their minds on the Chafee amendment, it is plausible that, in the absence of the usual outside information, many decided on the basis of what they heard in the floor debate. It seems that in terms of eloquence and logic, the argument between the Chafee and the anti-Chafee forces was a standoff, and so a typical senator might well have paid special attention to colleagues who seemed best qualified to judge the matter. Here, perhaps, is where Senator Chafee gained his decisive advantage. Speaking in favor of the Chafee amendment were the only two members who had come to the Senate from a career in academia, Senators Hayakawa of California and Moynihan of New York. Moreover, Senator Williams, the chairman of the committee responsible for the bill, also spoke in favor of Chafee's amendment. In the end, Cranston's substitute amendment was narrowly defeated. Having thus accepted the Chafee position, the Senate passed the bill by a decisive margin.

## Final Action

The legislative process now entered its final phase. A committee of Senate and House members was charged with drafting an acceptable compromise between the conflicting bills adopted earlier by the two houses.

At this point, strong opposition to the Chafee amendment developed in the higher education community. The AAUP opposed exempting college teachers from an MRA standard that applied to all other workers. The AAUP was prepared to affirm mandatory retirement in principle, as it had in earlier years, but it rejected the view that colleges and universities should have the right to impose an MRA of sixty-five at a time when the trend of public opinion and national legislation was to extend the upper limit to seventy. The Rhode Island chapter of the AAUP sent its executive director to Washington to meet Senators Chafee and Claiborne Pell and Congressman Edward Beard, all from Rhode Island. So intense was the AAUP's opposition that the Chafee amendment might well have been defeated, either in the Senate or in committee, had the timing of its introduction not been so unusual.

Although the conferees were not in a position to scrap the Chafee amendment altogether, they did limit the period of the exemption. Institutions would have the option to force retirement of faculty members at age sixty-five, but only until July 1, 1982. This action left open the possibility that Congress might later vote to extend the exemption beyond 1982. When the deadline arrived, however, there was no impetus to do so, and the exemption lapsed. Shortly before final congressional action, the AAUP gathered some evidence on the magnitude of the effects of raising the mandatory retirement age, but too late to have any impact (American Association of University Professors, 1978).

## Into the 1980s

Republicans won the 1980 presidential election and gained control of the Senate, changing somewhat the political environment for proposed changes in the ADEA. The change in partisan control, however, did not retard the pace of change in age-discrimination legislation. The Republican commitment to abolishing mandatory retirement was one of long standing. President Reagan affirmed his administration's position: to favor prohibiting employers from firing a worker because of age, but to oppose the elimination of age-seventy barriers in hiring, promotions, and other terms and conditions of employment (U.S. House of Representatives, 1982b). Soon after that, newly installed secretary of labor Raymond Donovan reaffirmed the administration's support for protecting current employees from forced retirement at age seventy. Donovan promised "vigorous efforts to secure passage of legislation during this session of Congress" (U.S. House of Representatives, 1982a, p. 8). Again, however, the Department of Labor's support was for legislation cast in the narrower frame already described. The president's statements diminished his influence on this issue, although it was important that Reagan supported the end of age-based mandatory retirement.

Events elsewhere in Washington helped focus attention on the need for additional age-discrimination legislation: The Department of Labor released a report on the impact of age discrimination in employment legislation (U.S. Department of Labor, 1982). Although the report did not endorse any new legislation, proponents of uncapping embraced it as evidence supporting their position. Finally, in the Republican-controlled Senate, the chair of the Senate Special Committee on Aging—a committee with considerable influence on age-related matters, although without authority to propose actual legislation—went to John Heinz of Pennsylvania, a politician prominently identified with a variety of age-related issues.

These events augmented existing support for uncapping, including that of Representative Pepper—now the oldest member of Congress, and widely respected as the spokesman for the age-rights cause. The AARP, with a membership of more than 25 million and a large financial base, also wielded substantial political influence.

All these influences kept total uncapping on the national governmental agenda, while Pepper and Heinz moved quickly to transform the matter from a policy option into actual legislation. On June 10, 1982, H.R. 6576 (the Pepper bill) and S.2617 (the Heinz bill) were simultaneously introduced in the House and Senate. Later that summer, hearings on uncapping were held by the House Select Committee on Aging, the Subcommittee on Employment Opportunities of the House Education and Labor Committee, and the Subcommittee on Labor of the Senate Labor and Human Resources Committee. The witnesses who appeared before these bodies fell into a regular pattern: the assistant secretary of labor, Malcolm Lovell; Pepper and Heinz; representatives of various organizations, in particular the AARP, the Gray Panthers, and the National Council on the Aging; and private citizens, usually themselves older people who had experienced age discrimination.

Although most testimony favored uncapping, some witnesses—most often representing higher education—opposed it. The AAUP, having recently completed a major reassessment of its own policy on this issue (AAUP, 1982), went on record as opposing legislation to uncap the mandatory retirement age. This left unchanged the AAUP governing council's 1978 position, which, while holding to its long-standing view that mandatory retirement at a predefined age works to the benefit of faculty and administrators alike, opposed any exemption from federal legislation.

This position differed from that of other higher educational organizations, most of which favored exemption. Nevertheless, all these groups, the AAUP included, united in written testimony to Congress that was delivered at the 1982 hearings. Representing the business community, the U.S. Chamber of Commerce also expressed its opposition to uncapping, more forcefully in these hearings than it had in those of 1977-78.

While opposition to total uncapping from higher education and the Chamber of Commerce was significant, by itself it could not have successfully thwarted congressional action at this point. More important were the deteriorating state of the economy during the 1981-83 recession, a high unemployment rate, and the consequent reluctance of organized labor to support legislative proposals that would benefit older workers to the possible detriment of younger ones. An informant on Capitol Hill at the time recalls attending a meeting in early 1983 on the pending social security amendments. "Claude Pepper was there," the informant recalls, "and Lane Kirkland, the AFL-CIO President, along with other members of the President's Commission on Social Security. Someone proposed that we should tie the idea of uncapping mandatory retirement as a kind of 'sweetener' to boosts in tax rates and the cut in social security benefits that were going to be necessary. People around the table began to show an interest in the idea. At first Kirkland was quiet, and then he said, 'I'm not sure that this is the best time for us to do this.' That was all he said, but it was enough to kill the idea." Presumably the labor federation, concerned over widespread joblessness and the fear that uncapping would adversely affect the job prospects of its members, let it be known through its lobbyists that proposals for uncapping at this juncture were not in labor's interest. If so, such a message would have carried weight, especially among liberal Democrats.

**Renewal of the Crusade**

By 1984, a new force had entered the picture, and it would lead at last to successful congressional action. This was a powerful coalition of municipal government officials and leaders of national firefighters' and police officers' associations. The 1978 amendments to the ADEA allowed certain employers to retire workers if such a practice could be considered a bona fide occupational qualification (BFOQ). States and municipalities around the country had used this exemption to continue the long-standing practice of forcing the retirement of firefighters and police officers—often at age fifty-five, although the established age varied among jurisdictions. The police and fire unions supported this practice, because it allowed them to argue for an enhanced early retirement package.

Notwithstanding the contrary views of their national unions, a number of affected public safety officers filed suit in federal court in the late 1970s, claiming that their forced retirement did not conform to any BFOQ. They maintained that no objective study had been undertaken to prove that job performance in their line of work declines measurably with advancing age. Because the courts did not always decide these cases in the same way, it was several years before local municipalities and unions appreciated the potential threat to mandatory retirement practices posed by these age-discrimination suits. After several unfavorable court judgments against them, the nation's organized municipalities and police and fire unions demanded a legislative clarification that would guarantee local governments the right to retire their public safety officers. This pressure gained urgency when, in 1985, the United States Supreme Court ruled that the City of Baltimore could not maintain its forced retirement policy under the BFOQ exemption.

Pressure on Congress to amend the ADEA also came from the U.S. Chamber of Commerce, which was deeply concerned about the effects of two provisions in the 1967 ADEA. One provision allowed double damage awards against employers in cases of willful age discrimination; the other allowed for jury trials—rather than bench hearings—in age-discrimination cases, which was the method provided for under the 1964 Civil Rights Act. The business community had found that jury trials generally worked to its disadvantage. The Chamber of Commerce felt that double damage awards and jury trials were resulting in unfair and extremely burdensome judgments against business firms.

It was ironic that these two forces—one demanding the right to continue the mandatory retirement of public safety officers, and the other restricting certain types of damage awards—finally succeeded in firing up the legislative engine behind the Pepper bill to uncap the MRA. While Pepper opposed all exemptions and special protections, he now seized this opportunity for renewed action. Pepper persuaded the House Committee on Education and Labor to schedule hearings on uncapping before the House Subcommittee on Employment Opportunities, both in 1984 and again in 1986. Partly because Pepper insisted that involuntary retirement should be permissible only on the basis of performance evaluation, in which affected workers were entitled to plead their case, the bill as it emerged from the full Education and Labor Committee provided no exceptions. As a concession to the police officers and firefighters, however, committee members proposed that the bill be debated in the full House under a rule allowing for amendment during floor debate. The amendment attached at that time, known as the Martinez amendment, granted a seven-year exemption to firefighters and police officers. Pepper voted against the Martinez amendment, and it appears from his remarks at the time that he believed he could persuade a majority of his House colleagues to vote accordingly. He was disappointed, however. The Martinez amendment was approved by a large margin. The House, by unanimous vote, approved the amended bill and sent it on to the Senate. Thus, the measure contained only a temporary exemption for police officers and firefighters and included neither the changes advocated by the Chamber of Commerce nor an exemption for higher education.

## The Issue Before the Senate

The Chamber of Commerce was not pleased with the legislation as it came before the Senate. Its lobbyists hoped that the Republican-controlled Senate would look more favorably than the Democrat-dominated House had on its particular requirements. Working with several conservative, probusiness senators, the Chamber of Commerce arranged for a series of legislative holds to be placed on the pending measure. Under Senate rules, the effect of a hold is to prevent a piece of legislation from being brought to the floor out of its sequence on the Senate calendar. The pressure of time in that body seldom permits consideration of all bills in one session; for this reason, much noncontroversial legislation is brought directly to the Senate floor under unanimous consent. Unless removed by the senator who placed it, a hold negates unanimous consent. The practical effect of the hold in this instance would be to kill the House-passed bill. The Chamber of Commerce also knew, as did proponents of uncapping, that if the House-passed bill went through the regular Senate committee structure, it would be amended in line with business's wishes or, failing that, buried entirely. It appeared, for the moment, that the Chamber of Commerce's lobbyists would be able to block the legislation.

But the Chamber of Commerce miscalculated. Its leaders failed to understand that the hold did not totally block unanimous consent, and that Senator Heinz and the AARP lobbyists were prepared to use all their legislative skills and resources to ensure that the House-passed bill went directly to the Senate floor, bypassing the regular committee structure. The AARP found out quickly which senators had applied the holds. Over the years, the AARP had effectively educated its members on this matter; therefore, in each of these senators' states, a cadre of politically aware members was prepared to lobby. Making this influence felt was not easy, since senators with strong probusiness outlooks do not move easily from established positions that they believe are important to U.S. business. Nevertheless, one by one the recalcitrants fell away, withdrawing their holds on the pending measure. The last one did not relent until the evening of the day the Senate was scheduled to adjourn.

Earlier that summer, the Senate Special Committee on Aging, chaired by Senator Heinz, had published a report (U.S. Senate, 1986) in which the committee compellingly presented the case for the pending measure. Now, Heinz arranged a series of closed-door meetings where a bipartisan group of senators who favored uncapping could explain their views.

Heinz, in persuading more than one reluctant senator of his own party, also made clear his position as chair of the Senate Republican Campaign Committee. He did not threaten to cut off campaign funding, but a reminder of his position nevertheless had its effect. Thus, a group of very conservative senators displayed their instincts for political survival, recognizing the logic of not appearing to oppose what one AARP lobbyist characterized as the greatest civil rights legislation for the elderly in the past twenty years.

As the legislative struggle drew to a close, the American Council on Education pressed for a fifteen-year exemption, which would be designed to ease out of the tenured ranks the large "bulge" of faculty members who initially had been recruited into academe in the 1960s and who were scheduled to retire in large numbers only in the late 1990s and beyond. Pepper, with little difficulty, initially had turned back all such bids for special exemptions. As before, the ACE lobbyists' chief contact in the Senate was Moynihan, although on this occasion they also had support from Senator Orrin Hatch of Utah. The higher education community might have been rebuffed in the Senate except that now higher education could be included in the seven-year exemption for public safety employees. The decision was a compromise, after lengthy and often frustrating negotiations between those who opposed any exemption and those who favored a permanent one. The seven-year rule was then offered to the higher education lobby on a take-it-or-leave-it basis. The seven-year tenured-faculty exemption made no particular sense from the standpoint of the "faculty bulge," but the senators believed that the colleges and universities deserved something, and this at least would represent a gesture in their direction.

All along, the AAUP had maintained that the changing MRA rules should be regarded as an economywide labor-allocation matter, rather than as a civil rights issue. The AAUP stated its concern that the twenty thousand additional workers the Department of Labor estimated would be added to the U.S. work force by uncapping would diminish the availability of jobs for young adults seeking entry-level employment. AAUP lobbyists also called attention to recent studies documenting the substantial numbers of recent college graduates unable to find employment appropriate to their level of education. Uncapping, the AAUP insisted, would have adverse effects for all younger workers, with younger faculty members and recent Ph.D. recipients not the least among them. Unlike the ACE and other institutional representatives, the AAUP maintained its opposition to any exemption for faculty members, on the basis that college and university instructors should be treated in the same fashion as others are in the U.S. work force. The final outcome, then, was a total rejection of AAUP views.

The 1986 debates brought to the fore another national organization, the American Federation of Teachers (AFT), whose representatives had not been especially prominent in the 1978 struggle. While the bulk of the AFT's membership consists of teachers in primary and secondary schools, the organization also includes a number of college and university teachers. Because these members are heavily concentrated in the New York City area, the organization has a degree of leverage over congressional delegations from that area. Furthermore, as a member union within the AFL/CIO, the AFT presumably had some influence with the more labor-oriented members of both houses of Congress. In marked opposition to other higher education groups, the AFT supported the proposed uncapping legislation. It is debatable whether the AFT commanded the prestige and political resources available to the more established lobby groups in higher education, but its position was helpful to those aligned with Pepper and Heinz in their efforts to refute the stands taken by the other national associations in this field.

**Final Action**

The 1986 amendments to the ADEA were passed in final form by both houses of Congress in late October of 1986, and President Reagan signed them into law on November 1. The only exemptions were for local public safety officers (police and fire) and tenured college and university professors, who would be exempted only until January 1, 1994. While Congress could vote to extend the exemptions or make them permanent, the mood on Capitol Hill indicated that the issue of mandatory retirement had at last been firmly settled.

**Conclusion**

Lobbyists for higher education did not greatly affect the ultimate resolution to uncap the MRA. Concessions made by lawmakers to higher education in 1978 and in 1986 amounted to symbolic gestures. Why the nation's higher education lobby had so little apparent influence in this case bears scrutiny. To a considerable degree, the higher education community was internally divided. At least three different positions were reflected in the official statements of national organizations, as well as in the positions of individuals and factions within these organizations.

One position held that mandatory retirement at age seventy protects the tenure system and guarantees dignified, nonprejudicial withdrawal from active service. A second view held that protection of mandatory retirement is unimportant in the long run but is still required for short-run reasons related to the hiring "bulge." Finally, some viewed uncapping as a civil rights matter, and therefore as one that called for a uniform national law allowing no one to be mandatorily retired for reasons unrelated to performance.

On none of these positions did the academic community achieve the consensus necessary for successful political intervention. The inability of lobbyists for individual groups in higher education to obtain more than symbolic reassurances should not be attributed to any lack of skill or perseverance on their part, however. Instead, the outcome reflected the enormous strength of the forces allied on the other side, as well as the fairly weak resolve on the part of higher education's own constituents and organizations.

## References

Abrams, M., and Robinson, B. (eds.). *Forty-Six National Leaders Speak Out on Options for Older Americans*. Washington, D.C.: National Retired Teachers Association and American Association of Retired Persons, 1971.
Altman, J. "Social Security: The Worst Is Yet to Come." *New York Times*, July 9, 1977, p. 17.
American Association of University Professors. "Academic Retirement and Related Subjects." *AAUP Bulletin*, 1950, *36* (1), 97-117.
American Association of University Professors. "Report of the Council Committee on Discrimination." *AAUP Bulletin*, 1972, *58* (2), 160-163.
American Association of University Professors. "The Impact of Federal Retirement-Age Legislation on Higher Education." *AAUP Bulletin*, 1978, *65* (4), 319-330.
American Association of University Professors. "Uncapping the Mandatory Retirement Age." *Academe*, 1982, *68* (5), 14a-18a.
Ford, L. C. "The Implications of the Age Discrimination in Employment Act Amendments of 1978 for Colleges and Universities." *Journal of College and University Law*, 1978-79, *5* (3), 161-209.
Johnson, L. B. "Special Message to the Congress Proposing Programs for Older Americans: January 23, 1967." In Johnson, L. B., *Public Papers of Lyndon B. Johnson*, Vol. 1. Washington, D.C.: U.S. Government Printing Office, 1967.
"Private Colleges Seek Balanced Student Aid, Stabilized Enrollment." *Chronicle of Higher Education*, February 22, 1977, p. 10.
Schuck, P. H. "The Graying of Civil Rights Law." *The Public Interest*, Summer 1980, pp. 69-93.
U.S. Congress. *Congressional Record-Senate, October 19, 1977*. Washington, D.C.: U.S. Government Printing Office, 1977.
U.S. Department of Labor. *The Older American Worker: Age Discrimination in Employment*. Washington, D.C.: U.S. Department of Labor, 1965.
U.S. Department of Labor. *Final Report to Congress on Age Discrimination in Employment Act Studies*. Washington, D.C.: Department of Labor, 1982.
U.S. House of Representatives, Committee on Education and Labor, Subcommittee on Employment Opportunities. *Hearing to Eliminate Mandatory Retirement*. Washington, D.C.: U.S. Government Printing Office, 1982a.
U.S. House of Representatives, Select Committee on Aging. *Mandatory Retirement: The Social and Human Costs of Forced Idleness*. Washington, D.C.: U.S. Government Printing Office, 1977.
U.S. House of Representatives, Select Committee on Aging. *The End of Mandatory Retirement: Hearings*. Washington, D.C.: U.S. Government Printing Office, 1982b.

U.S. Senate, Committee on Human Resources. *Report: Amending the Age Discrimination in Employment Amendments of 1977.* Washington, D.C.: U.S. Government Printing Office, 1977.

U.S. Senate, Special Committee on Aging. *Working Americans: Equality at Any Age.* Washington, D.C.: U.S. Government Printing Office, 1986.

White House Conference on Aging. *Policy Statements and Recommendations.* Washington, D.C.: U.S. Department of Health, Education and Welfare, 1961.

White House Conference on Aging. *Section Recommendations on Employment and Retirement.* Washington, D.C.: U.S. Government Printing Office, 1971.

*Henry J. Pratt is professor of political science at Wayne State University and faculty associate, Wayne State Institute of Gerontology.*

*Raising the mandatory retirement age from sixty-five to seventy is estimated to have relatively small, short-term effects on the retirement timing of tenured faculty members.*

# Retirement Behavior and Mandatory Retirement in Higher Education

*Karen C. Holden, W. Lee Hansen*

The 1978 amendments to the ADEA, which raised the legal minimum age of mandatory retirement to seventy, included a three-year exemption that permitted universities and colleges to continue to retire tenured faculty members mandatorily as early as age sixty-five. The 1978 amendments also ordered the U.S. Department of Labor to examine the labor-force effects of an MRA change (U.S. Department of Labor, 1982). The results discussed in this chapter are from a study commissioned by the Department of Labor to examine the effects of the increase in mandatory retirement age on tenured college faculty members and their institutions (Hansen and Holden, 1981).

An MRA is only one of many factors that influence the age at which faculty members retire. To assess the net effect of MRA policies alone, it is necessary to undertake a more comprehensive study of why faculty members retire when they do. Four questions guided the research presented in this chapter:

1. What was the prevalence and meaning of an MRA in higher education?

2. What was the relative influence of pension and MRA policies on the age when faculty members retired?
3. What were the likely direct, first-round effects of raising the MRA?
4. What were the most effective ways of encouraging faculty members to consider retiring earlier?

We begin by outlining the historical connection between pension and MRA policies in higher education. Next, we report our findings on how mandatory retirement affects the timing of retirement for individual faculty members, and we then use these estimates to simulate the effects of delays in retirement on institutional costs and new hires.

**Pension and MRA Policies in Higher Education**

The evolution of mandatory retirement practices in higher education cannot be understood without reference to the development of pension plans and the role they have played in determining the provisions and administration of personnel practices (Greenough, 1948; Greenough and King, 1969; King and Cook, 1980). A key element in this development was the concept of tenure, which came to be inextricably linked with support of mandatory retirement practices by the major higher educational organizations.

These links were formalized in 1950, when the American Association of University Professors (AAUP), an organization created early in this century to prevent dismissal of professors because of their social or political views, and the Association of American Colleges (AAC) jointly issued a statement strongly supportive of MRA limits. This joint statement recommended that MRAs be well defined, fixed, and set between the ages of sixty-five and seventy, after which time faculty members could begin receiving pension benefits (American Association of University Professors, 1950a, 1950b). A 1969 statement reaffirmed the 1950 MRA recommendations (American Association of University Professors, 1969).

Colleges and universities have patterned their retirement provisions in conformity with AAUP-AAC recommendations, as indicated by the high percentage of institutions with an MRA and, before the 1978 amendments, the high percentage that set the MRA between sixty-five and seventy (Table 1). The widespread presence of an MRA is also consistent with the prevalence of tenure: The majority of institutions, employing almost 92 percent of all full-time faculty members forty-five and older, have tenure systems.

The singling out by Congress of tenured faculty members, subjecting all other employees in institutions of higher education to the ADEA, was an implicit recognition by Congress of the link between MRA practices and tenure. While concern about raising the MRA most often focused on its monetary impact and consequent reductions in job openings and

Table 1. Distribution of Higher Education Institutions by MRA Provisions, 1978[a]

| Type of Institution | No MRA | Percent of institutions with MRA=65 | MRA=66–69 | MRA=70+ | Distribution of 1980 Faculty[b] |
|---|---|---|---|---|---|
| Private | 14.9 | 67.3 | 2.4 | 15.4 | 23.1% |
| University | 0.0 | 67.2 | 12.4 | 20.4 | 6.0 |
| Four-Year | 11.8 | 71.8 | 2.0 | 14.4 | 15.5 |
| Two-Year | 44.9 | 34.8 | 0.0 | 20.3 | 0.7 |
| Public | 17.9 | 55.8 | 8.9 | 17.2 | 76.9 |
| University | 3.2 | 45.0 | 14.8 | 37.0 | 21.4 |
| Four-Year | 5.2 | 44.9 | 15.7 | 34.8 | 29.5 |
| Two-Year | 25.8 | 62.3 | 5.0 | 6.8 | 26.0 |
| Total | 16.5 | 61.1 | 6.0 | 16.4 | 100.0 |

[a] Based on weighted responses from 278 institutions.
[b] Full-time faculty only, all ages.

promotions, the larger threat was to the broad support for tenure among faculty and administrators in a period of diminishing employment opportunities. Still, little or no data were available about the effect on retirement patterns of the 1978 ADEA amendments, and this deficiency led to the special Department of Labor study.

In 1980, we undertook a two-stage survey of institutions and their tenured faculty members. We first sent a questionnaire to institutions of higher education, stratified according to type (public or private), size, and degrees granted, to obtain information on recent retirements, enrollments, pension plans, and other fringe benefits. We then drew a sample of faculty members at the responding institutions and sent them a questionnaire to obtain information on expected retirement age, current work activity, salary level, and other personal characteristics, as well as publication records, information on assets, and related matters. Only faculty members fifty or older were asked to complete the questionnaire.

This method of surveying faculty members allowed us to match faculty and institutional data and, by knowing the specific retirement policies of each institution, to avoid the problems that would have been created when individuals were unable to provide all the complex information we requested. Responses to both surveys came primarily from universities and four-year colleges and their faculty members. We can only speculate why so few two-year colleges responded; perhaps they were less likely to have formal tenure systems or any MRA and thus had less motivation to respond to a survey on an issue of no great concern to them. With this exception, the distribution of respondents—both institutions and faculty members—by type of institution, and between the private and public sectors, represented their respective national populations.

## Mandatory Retirement Policies in Higher Education

Our 1980 surveys revealed the prevalence of MRAs of sixty-five and seventy, as well as changes that were already under way in anticipation of the 1982 expiration date of the tenured-faculty exemption. Because institutions with large numbers of faculty members were primarily public colleges and universities, where the MRA was most likely to be age seventy, the distribution of institutions and faculty by MRA is different. Thus, while almost two-thirds of institutions maintained an MRA of sixty-five before the 1978 amendments, only a slight majority (51 percent) of all full-time faculty members faced an MRA of sixty-five at that time (Table 2). By 1980, several states had already raised or abolished the MRA, pushing the percentage of faculty members facing an MRA of sixty-five down to 32 percent; MRAs between ages sixty-six and sixty-nine had almost disappeared.

The pace of adjustment differed considerably between the public and private sectors. Public institutions were less likely than private institutions to use the exemption, partly because public institutions had to conform to state retirement laws that preempted the federal exemption. At the time of our survey, approximately half of all public institutions—but only a quarter of all private institutions—with an MRA of sixty-five in 1978 had raised it to age seventy. Relatively few private institutions eliminated the MRA. Even when states did provide a faculty exemption, inclusion of all public employees in the same retirement programs usually required similar treatment of faculty members and nonexempt employees.

Table 2. Distribution of 1980 Full-Time Faculty by MRA Program in 1978 and 1980[a]

| Type of Institution | No MRA | MRA=65 | MRA=66-69 | MRA=70+ |
|---|---|---|---|---|
| *Based on 1978 MRA Provisions* | | | | |
| Private | 3.8 | 77.1 | 6.9 | 12.6 |
| Public | 7.9 | 43.2 | 17.3 | 31.6 |
| Total | 7.0 | 50.9 | 14.9 | 27.1 |
| *Based on 1980 MRA Provisions* | | | | |
| Private | 5.2 | 56.3 | 6.1 | 32.5 |
| Public | 14.5 | 25.3 | 3.4 | 56.9 |
| Total | 12.4 | 32.3 | 4.0 | 51.3 |

[a]Based on full-time faculty members reported by 268 institutions; excludes ten institutions that reported no full-time faculty members.

The survey revealed one important surprise: Mandatory retirement did not uniformly mean that faculty members could not continue full-time employment past the MRA. Rather, many institutions applied their MRA policies with considerable flexibility, permitting year-to-year extensions of teaching service at institutional discretion. Moreover, private institutions, while less likely to have an MRA of seventy, were far more likely to report extension policies and to specify no upper age limit on these extensions. Only 13 percent of institutions with an MRA of sixty-five reported a no-extension policy, compared to 40 percent with an MRA of seventy. Limited extensions to age seventy were available at 26 percent of the institutions with an MRA of sixty-five, while the remaining 51 percent set no age limit. Thus, the actual or effective MRA proved to be higher than an official MRA of sixty-five would have seemed to indicate.

Because of the frequent coupling of an MRA of sixty-five with flexible extension policies, the mandated switch to an MRA of seventy did not so much represent a rise in the maximum age beyond which faculty members could no longer be employed as it did a change in who could decide whether to extend employment. A flexible MRA of sixty-five is distinctly different from a typically inflexible MRA of seventy. With a lower MRA, extensions were not automatic; rather, they were individually negotiated arrangements that could take into consideration the abilities of individual faculty members as well as institutional needs. The key distinction between an MRA of sixty-five and an MRA of seventy was not the prohibition of employment beyond age sixty-five; it was who decided when an individual had to retire.

## Faculty Response to MRA Policies

Concerns about the economic effects of a higher MRA centered on the assumption that faculty members would retire later, if permitted to do so. In light of the flexibility of MRA policies—that is, the ability of many faculty members, even before the 1978 amendments, to continue working at least to age seventy—what remained unclear was how many faculty members might be expected to delay retirement and the effect of such delay on universities and colleges.

We used two approaches to resolve these questions. First, we examined differences in the age at which faculty member retired during the 1978–79 academic year at institutions with MRAs of sixty-five and seventy. Second, using faculty survey data, we tried to isolate the effects of an MRA of sixty-five on retirement timing from the effects of other factors that might cause retirement rates to be different across institutions.

On the basis of data that institutions provided about the age distribution of their full-time faculty members in 1979–80 and about retirements in the previous academic year, we calculated retirement rates for faculty members by age. These rates measured the percentages of the retirement-age faculty who retired during the 1979–80 academic year. Our estimates indicated that retirements before age sixty-five from institutions in our sample were surprisingly infrequent. Even at institutions with an MRA of sixty-five, only 60 percent of the affected faculty members actually retired. More important, both public and private institutions with an MRA of sixty-five reported significantly higher retirement rates of faculty members between ages sixty-five and sixty-nine. Moreover, retirement rates were significantly lower in private than in public institutions under an MRA of either sixty-five or seventy, which indicated that factors other than MRA policies were influencing differences in retirement ages between the public and private sectors.

Our second approach to examining the effect of MRA provisions on the retirement behavior of faculty members came from an analysis of the determinants of expected retirement age, based on data from our faculty respondents. The use of expected (rather than actual) retirement age was necessitated by the absence of information on faculty retirees' characteristics and on the opportunities open to them when they decided to retire. We cannot, of course, be certain that expected retirement ages will ever be realized, but evidence suggests that older workers predict their actual retirement ages quite closely (see Burkhauser and Quinn, this volume; Reimers, 1977; Hansen and Holden, 1981). Table 3 shows expected retire-

Table 3. Average Expected Retirement Age by 1980 MRA

|  | Mandatory Retirement Age | |
| --- | --- | --- |
| Current Age | 65 | 70 |
| 56–59 | | |
| Public | 65.7 | 65.3 |
| Private | 67.6 | 67.8 |
| 60–61 | | |
| Public | 66.0 | 66.3 |
| Private | 67.5 | 65.8 |
| 62 | | |
| Public | 65.6 | 66.4 |
| Private | 66.2 | 66.0 |
| 63–64 | | |
| Public | 65.6 | 66.8[a] |
| Private | 66.8 | 69.0[b] |
| 56–64 | | |
| Public | 65.7 | 65.9 |
| Private | 67.3 | 67.5 |

[a] Difference in expected age between MRA groups is significant at 0.01 level.
[b] Difference in expected age between MRA groups is significant at 0.05 level.

ment ages, distinguished by respondents' ages and the MRA and by the public or private status of their colleges or universities. The late expected age of their retirement confirms the conclusions we drew from our data on the institutions. Even with an MRA of sixty-five, faculty members on average expect to retire after age sixty-five. The influence of the lower MRA was evident only for the older group, whose retirement might take place before the exemption expired. Further, faculty members in private institutions expected to retire somewhat later.

A fixed MRA, however, is only one way of encouraging retirement at a particular age. Other important factors are the financial incentives provided through pension plans, the possibilities of supplementing retirement income through other activities, and any special early-retirement incentives. Pension plans can be structured to provide targeted retirement benefits at an earlier or later age than the MRA, with greater or lesser gains in benefit amounts if participants continue to work. In 1980, for example, some institutions ceased or reduced employers' contributions to pension plans and the crediting of years of service beyond the normal retirement age. In this situation, faculty members would gain less financially from contining to work than from being at institutions where employers' contributions and credit for service continued. Salaries, which also determine the total pension benefit available at normal retirement age, may also increase at rates that signal to faculty members how their institutions view their continued employment. In short, institutions that want to encourage retirement at age sixty-five can do so in ways other than through an MRA. When faculty members respond to these other incentives, an MRA may be irrelevant to their retirement planning, even though simple correlations indicate that where an MRA of sixty-five exists, faculty do retire earlier.

Because our survey provided information on the characteristics of individual faculty members and on the structures of pension programs at their colleges or universities, we were able to separate the influence on retirement timing of MRA provisions from other factors. The central feature of our analysis is its ability to focus on the effects of mandatory retirement while controlling for other financial variables. We constructed estimates not only of the size of the pension that each individual would receive at a particular age but also of the present value of the pension annuity over his or her expected lifetime. (See Chapter Five for a numerical example of this argument.)

We did this by using information provided by institutions on actual pension provisions, as well as information provided by faculty members on current compensation and years of coverage in defined-benefit plans or total contributions in defined-contribution (such as TIAA) plans. We controlled for changes in the present value of the benefits available to each faculty member at age sixty-five if retirement were delayed by one year, since we assumed that the greater this gain, the more likely a faculty member would be to choose delayed retirement. From each faculty member, we obtained total accumulations in TIAA-CREF plans, including contributions to tax-deferred annuities. We knew the institution's contribution rate and calculated the annuity payable at different ages. If the member was covered by a state plan, we asked for total years of service and, with data on current institutional salaries, were then able to estimate benefits, using known state formulas and projected salary increases. Faculty members covered by other plans had their anticipated benefits calculated in a like manner. Estimated retirement income was discounted to age sixty-five by a 5 percent discount rate, plus an assumed 10 percent inflation rate adjusted for any automatic inflation (or investment earnings) adjustments built into the plans.

Several other financial characteristics likely to affect retirement decisions were also controlled in this analysis: social security coverage, current salary levels, and professional income from other sources. To test the view that the professional contributions of faculty members affect their retirement plans—and, hence, that delayed retirement is most likely among the most productive faculty members—we included indicators of productivity, measured by books and articles published in the past three years and by current involvement in publishable research. The questions were phrased in such a way that artistic performances and exhibitions could also be counted.

The results of our analysis are summarized here; complete results are given in Hansen and Holden (1981). We focus on two separate age groups, fifty-six to sixty-one and sixty-two to sixty-four. We treat these groups separately because members of the younger group may have already adjusted their retirement plans by the time of our survey, since they knew then that an MRA of sixty-five could no longer be enforced by the time they reached retirement age. Most of the older group would reach age sixty-five before the exemption ended; therefore, we assumed that MRA provisions in force at their institutions in 1980 were relevant to their reported retirement expectations.

Even after controlling for financial, institutional, and personal characteristics, we found that an MRA of sixty-five exerted a significant and negative effect on the expected retirement age of older faculty members, although (as we had anticipated) it did not affect the retirement plans of those under sixty-two. An MRA of sixty-five alone reduced the anticipated retirement age by just over one year compared to an MRA of seventy. Differences existed in retirement expectations among older faculty, with an anticipated retirement age almost two years later in private as compared to public institutions. This finding is perplexing, since any difference due to pensions (especially any difference between public and TIAA plans) should be controlled by the pension-value variables. It is possible that unmeasured differences in work environments and in anticipated salary and benefit increases play some role.

Pension variables had little effect on when faculty members expected to retire. Current salary mattered most to the younger group, while professional income beyond basic institutional salary mattered most to the older group. This other income might be from medical-practice fees, outside consulting, additional earnings from summer school, or book royalties—all of which are not included in basic salary. For both age groups, higher financial rewards were associated with later expected retirement. These compensation variables indicate how institutions and outside groups alike reward faculty members who are the most valued in their profession. Among younger faculty members, involvement in current research and greater publishing activity increased expected retirement age. This was not the case for older faculty members, a finding that indicates either that there is greater emphasis on research productivity among younger faculty members or that the least productive faculty members had already retired (hence, they were not included in our older sample).

How do we interpret these findings? We know from these and other data that, on the average, tenured faculty members intend to and do retire at age sixty-five or later. Older respondents in our survey were more likely to anticipate later retirement. While this finding may indicate that as faculty members age, they become more reluctant to retire, it may also reflect selective attrition before the time of our study. Indeed, the evidence is fairly compelling that faculty members with fewer publications and lower salaries expect to retire earlier than their more productive colleagues do. Thus, delayed retirement by less productive faculty members may present a smaller problem than had been feared.

An MRA of sixty-five did influence retirement plans, but pension structures did not. This finding does not necessarily indicate that early-retirement incentives will not encourage earlier retirement. In fact, our survey indicated that few institutions offered meaningful early-retirement incentives, and so our results reflect only the normal pension gains from extended employment.

Two other findings deserve mention. Faculty members covered by social security anticipated significantly earlier retirement. This indicates that faculty members are not immune to financial considerations; the incentives built into social security, including the provision of benefits to spouses and widows, as well as inflation adjustments, play a major role in providing retirement security for faculty members. The unexpected positive influence of other professional income on retirement age—unexpected because we had anticipated that other sources of income would reduce ties to teaching and research—suggests that the faculty members who were the most heavily engaged in other activities depended on their institutional ties to obtain research grants, consulting contracts, speaking engagements, and other remunerative professional activities. But this variable may also indicate that faculty members whose contributions were the most valued, inside and outside their institutions, anticipated being able—and, when MRAs were in force, being invited—to extend employment well past an age when their less productive colleagues would retire.

### Estimates of the Cost Effects of a Change in the MRA

Any assessment of the impact on costs of changing the age of mandatory retirement must consider that many institutions (39 percent) did not have an MRA of sixty-five in 1978, and that an even larger percentage of faculty members were not subject to this early MRA (49 percent). Our results suggest that for faculty members subject to an MRA of sixty-five, a change to an MRA of seventy would, on the average, lead to a one-year delay in retirement. As this happened, later retirements would reduce new job openings among institutions planning to maintain the current size of their faculties. To the extent that these older faculty members received higher salaries than "displaced" new hires, total faculty compensation budgets would increase. The decline in new hires would be temporary, however, because eventually the delayed retirements would occur and raise retirement levels higher than they would have been. Meanwhile, the level of job openings would increase again. Cost increases would be long-term effects, however, because of the relatively higher salaries paid to faculty delaying retirement. If institutions were forced to hold total compensation costs constant, the temporary reduction in new hires would be even deeper, and faculty size would be slightly reduced in the long term.

Our survey information on faculty retirements from institutions with different MRAs proved useful in simulating the timing and magnitude of these effects. To estimate the impact of changing from an MRA of sixty-five to one of seventy, we developed an initial age profile of faculty members in institutions with an MRA of sixty-five. It was important to understand what pattern of costs and hires could be expected if institutions with an MRA of sixty-five were not required to change that policy. Only by comparing this case with our simulations that assume a change to an MRA of seventy is it possible to assess the net impact of the higher MRA. For our base estimates, we used the 1979–80 retention rates for faculty members at institutions with an MRA of sixty-five. We assumed constant faculty size and constant compensation budgets, to give structure to the simulation results. We simulated budget size and new hires to the year 2007. (The precise years are important only because we begin with 1979–80 faculty age structures.)

Lines 1-2 and 7-8 of Table 4 portray the course of events based on the assumption that an MRA of sixty-five continues. Even when the MRA does not change, institutions face financial stringency during the first few years of the simulation period. This is due in part to the payment of increasingly higher salaries to the large cohort of faculty members hired during the post-World War II expansion in higher education. Shortly after, however, that cohort begins to retire, and this factor increases the hiring rate for new faculty members well above that in the base period. If institutions are forced by constant-budget constraints to trim new hires even more than required by the fixed-faculty-size constraint, the later increase in the rate of new hires is greater (line 8). Note that by the last year of the constant-budget simulation, faculty size is actually larger than in the initial year, because of the lower costs resulting from the hiring of a relatively young and therefore less expensive faculty.

Next, we simulated the pattern of costs and hires if the MRA rises to seventy, employing alternative retention patterns—the pattern actually reported by institutions with an MRA of seventy—and a worst case pattern. Finally, we incorporated faculty members' expectations, to construct another alternative set of retention rates based on the expectations of faculty members then employed at institutions with an MRA of sixty-five. In Table 4, we present only the first two alternative scenarios, since the simulation based on faculty members' expectations fell midway between these two. In each case, the MRA is assumed to change to seventy in the third year of the simulation period—which is what happened. As can be seen from lines 3-4 and 9-10, salary costs rise only slightly (compared to the base case), and new hires fall by at most 2 percent. In both the constant-faculty case and the constant-budget case, new hires remain below the base case for most of the simulation period but recover by the end of the period.

Because the pattern of retirement we assumed under an MRA of seventy may not fully reflect the adjustments that faculty members eventually will make to the later retirement age, we simulated what would happen if three-quarters of all faculty members worked until age seventy. This admittedly arbitrary assumption seemed a reasonable representation of the worst-case fears of higher education, since some faculty members can always be expected to retire voluntarily or because of disability before reaching age seventy. In the constant-faculty-size case, we do see a precipitous drop in new hires immediately after the new MRA is in place (1987), and the level of new hires remains below that of the base case throughout the simulation period. Because the constant-budget case requires a far deeper cut in new hires during the first years, the number of new hires is actually higher than in the base case by 2007.

The age distributions of college and university faculties differ considerably, and so these "average" results may not be too meaningful. In our

Table 4. Index of Budget and New Hires with Faculty Size and Budget Held Constant[a]
(Different Retention Patterns)

| Retention Patterns | 1979 | 1982 | 1987 | 1992 | 1997 | 2002 | 2007 |
|---|---|---|---|---|---|---|---|
| | | | | *Faculty Size Held Constant* | | | |
| *MRA 65 Continues* | | | | | | | |
| 1. Budget size | 100.0 | 104.0 | 103.2 | 102.5 | 101.8 | 100.6 | 99.8 |
| 2. New hires | 100.0 | 53.9 | 106.1 | 104.2 | 100.0 | 107.9 | 106.1 |
| *MRA 70 Pattern* | | | | | | | |
| 3. Budget size | 100.0 | 104.0 | 103.3 | 102.7 | 102.0 | 100.8 | 100.0 |
| 4. New hires | 100.0 | 53.9 | 104.2 | 103.0 | 100.6 | 106.1 | 106.1 |
| *MRA 70: Worst Case* | | | | | | | |
| 5. Budget size | 100.0 | 104.0 | 105.8 | 105.6 | 104.7 | 103.1 | 101.6 |
| 6. New hires | 100.0 | 53.9 | 77.6 | 92.7 | 95.8 | 101.8 | 104.2 |
| | | | | *Budget Held Constant* | | | |
| *MRA 65 Continues* | | | | | | | |
| 7. Faculty size | 100.0 | 97.9 | 99.3 | 100.4 | 101.1 | 102.9 | 103.6 |
| 8. New hires | 100.0 | 41.8 | 114.5 | 109.7 | 101.2 | 117.0 | 108.5 |
| *MRA 70 Pattern* | | | | | | | |
| 9. Faculty size | 100.0 | 97.9 | 99.1 | 100.0 | 100.9 | 102.6 | 103.5 |
| 10. New hires | 100.0 | 41.8 | 112.1 | 107.9 | 103.0 | 115.2 | 109.1 |
| *MRA 70: Worst Case* | | | | | | | |
| 11. Faculty size | 100.0 | 97.9 | 95.6 | 96.4 | 98.0 | 100.4 | 102.6 |
| 12. New hires | 100.0 | 41.8 | 66.1 | 100.0 | 104.2 | 113.9 | 114.5 |

[a] 1979 = 100 in all retention patterns.

survey, wide variation existed across institutions in the percentage of faculty members then approaching retirement. Among all faculty members forty-five and older, the number who were between sixty and sixty-four varied from 1 to 27 percent. No discernible pattern appeared by type of institution or by age of mandatory retirement, although institutions with an MRA of sixty-five did have somewhat fewer faculty members between sixty-five and sixty-nine years old (3 percent versus 5 percent). While no particular type of institution was uniformly confronted either by an old or a young faculty, a few institutions were faced with a large percentage of older faculty members. This case was most likely for two-year institutions. Accordingly, we reran the simulations for different age distributions. The results (not shown here) indicated that for institutions with older age structures, budget costs could increase by an additional 2 percent, and hiring would drop by another 20 percent to 25 percent. (Again, the effects are concentrated in the transition period and later diminish.) Differences in age and salary profiles also influence the magnitude of the costs involved in adjusting to the change in the MRA. If we assume a more steeply rising salary profile than one that flattens out after ages fifty to fifty-four, budget costs rise by about another half of one percentage point, and new hiring drops slightly.

There is no easy way to add up the results of these various simulations. The base simulation shows how poorly timed the 1978 amendments were, coming precisely when colleges and universities were forced to sharply reduce new hires. The additional effects of the change in the MRA were concentrated in the period centering on 1987, and they later dissipated, which indicates that this one-time change produces a one-time (although delayed) effect. Under even the most severe assumptions about future retirement rates, and assuming constant faculty size, a rise in the MRA to seventy is estimated to raise faculty compensation costs to a level about 2.5 to 3.0 percent higher than in the base case. New hires bear the impact, dropping more than 40.0 percent in the worst case but then recovering to the level of the base case.

Taken together, the simulations suggest that the average impact of the rise in the MRA to seventy may have been to raise salary costs at most by 3 percent, with the cost of reductions in hiring falling selectively on more recent job-market entrants. It is they who will face (or have faced) a tight job market. Institutions with older age distributions and steeper age and salary profiles are likely to have experienced somewhat larger cost increases. Ten years after the change, however, cost differences across institutions with different age or salary profiles narrowed considerably. This is the one-time result, of course, of the change in the age of retirement from sixty-five to seventy. If, however, faculty members retire at the rates experienced by institutions that in 1980 already had an MRA of seventy, or at the rate expected by our faculty respondents, the impact will be far smaller, reducing faculty size by at most 3.0 percent in the constant-budget case or raising budgets by 2.1 percent in the constant-faculty-size case.

## Coping with Change

Our results indicate that, with increases in institutional costs and reductions in job openings, MRA changes alone are likely to delay the retirement of tenured faculty members, particularly those in private institutions. Some colleges and universities will be more able than others to offset temporary declines in anticipated job openings by allocating funds from other sources or by raising additional funds. Such adjustments are more difficult when they coincide with enrollment declines (and their associated reductions in revenues), reductions in state and federal funding for higher education, and a shift in enrollments among types of institutions or programs.

What policies can colleges and universities develop to adapt to the desire of faculty members to delay retirement? Changes in tenure contracts, periodic productivity reviews, salary freezes past some age, mid-career development programs, and early-retirement incentives have all been suggested for encouraging faculty members to retire earlier. Our research could not evaluate the effectiveness of these approaches. Because we were interested in the effect of financial variables on retirement behavior, however, we did ascertain the faculty members' responses to early-retirement incentive programs (ERIs).

ERIs attempt to make early retirement financially more attractive to faculty members. ERIs may apply across the board or selectively to programs or individuals. At the time of our survey, few institutions had extensive ERIs.

To learn more about how such incentives might work, we asked faculty respondents whether they would retire at an earlier age under three different financial plans. Early retirees would (1) receive the same pension benefits that they would have received at their expected age of retirement, (2) be allowed to reduce their academic responsibilities, with commensurate reductions in salary, or (3) have their pension benefits fully indexed for cost-of-living increases, beginning with their earlier retirement.

Because of the high average yearly inflation rate (10 percent) when our survey was conducted, we anticipated enthusiasm for the third option. Instead, 37 percent of the respondents said that the second option, which allowed for a phased retirement, was the most attractive, while 25 percent chose the first option and 22 percent chose the third. The remaining 16 percent were undecided or did not respond. Another major difference emerged when we looked at the expected retirement age of respondents. Those interested in the first and third options already anticipated retiring relatively early, while the second option proved as appealing to those who expected to retire early as to those who expected to retire late. In fact, the second option appeared most likely to accelerate the retirement of persons who had expected to delay retirement well past age sixty-five.

We simulated budget costs and new hires under the second and third early-retirement options, and retirement ages did change, as faculty members themselves had said they would. Fully indexed retirement benefits reduced salary costs slightly, compared to the pattern associated with the MRA of seventy; consequently, new hires were slightly higher. Budget costs remained 1 percent above the base level. Because the indexing of retirement benefits would entail additional costs (not included in our simulations), it is unlikely that any net gain would accrue to institutions.

The impact of phased retirement was considerably larger, reducing costs in 1987 and later pushing them below the base levels; consequently, new hires were at least equal to those in the base case. By definition, this result follows from the greater interest expressed by our sample in phased retirement (versus other early-retirement options) and from the earlier retirement of relatively higher-paid faculty members.

Initially, we were surprised by the popularity of phased retirement, especially since the survey was conducted in a period when salary increases lagged behind inflation and pensions were not indexed to inflation. Under these conditions, early retirement could be considered economically hazardous. A likely explanation is that the strong attachment to work expressed by the faculty members in our sample means that some type of institutional affiliation is necessary and desirable for them to continue their other professional work and interests. Phased retirement appears to guarantee that connection for a longer time.

## Conclusion

Shifting to an MRA of seventy was likely to delay the average age of retirement, which indicates that an MRA of sixty-five constrained the ability of faculty members to delay retirement unilaterally. The delay was not longer because MRA practices before the 1978 amendments were flexible, enabling about one-half of faculty members reaching age sixty-five to extend their employment beyond that age. Even with an MRA of sixty-five, the mean expected retirement age among those between sixty-two and sixty-four was close to sixty-seven.

When we simulated the effect of ADEA-induced delayed retirement on institutional costs and job openings, we found that personnel costs would rise by at most 3 percent, new openings would decrease sharply, and faculties would become progressively older and continue to be older than would otherwise have been the case. The institutions most affected by the change were private universities, where an MRA of sixty-five had been most prevalent and where faculty members expected to retire well past that age.

The finding that faculty members in higher education retire late, and therefore that a change in the MRA from sixty-five to seventy is more likely to influence their behavior, is not unique to our study. For example, a 1972-73 survey of TIAA-CREF annuitants showed that among male faculty, administrators, and staff, 83 percent had retired at age sixty-five or later (Mulanaphy, 1981). Corwin and Knepper (1978) also found from their 1977-78 data on actual retirements among faculty members that tenured faculty members were most likely to delay retirement to at least age sixty-four or sixty-five. Similarly, Ladd and Lipset (1977) found that among faculty members who expected to retire at age sixty or later, 90 percent planned to do so at sixty-four, at sixty-five, or later. Finally, a 1979 survey of faculty members at institutions participating in the Consortium on the Financing of Higher Education (see Chapter Four) indicated that almost 70 percent planned to retire at the MRA, which in most cases was sixty-five.

Nevertheless, these late anticipated retirement ages are not unchangeable, since faculty members in our survey expressed considerable interest in early-retirement incentive programs. It is possible that, while pension plan structures have little effect on the timing of retirement, ERIs offering large and sharp differences in benefits—at, say, age sixty-four as compared to age sixty-five—may be effective in stimulating earlier retirement. Moreover, ERIs that include continuing institutional affiliation are of the greatest interest and, according to our analysis, will have the largest accelerating effect on the date of planned retirement. At the same time, ERIs sufficient to induce retirement among those faculty members who do not yet want to retire must be carefully structured. On the average, we find the least productive faculty already planning earlier retirement. Thus, the introduction of ERIs may end up changing the retirement plans primarily of faculty members who are the most productive and highly rewarded people in their fields.

The short-run dilemma faced in 1982 by higher education was to adjust to the hiring squeeze that would have resulted even if an MRA of sixty-five had continued. To attribute those projected changes in retirement rates to changes in the MRA would be to exaggerate the impact of the latter. At the same time, a higher MRA alone would, over the long run, increase budget costs, as older faculty members delayed retirement and reduced their institutions' hiring flexibility. Additional costs were not likely to be overwhelming, especially salary costs, which are only a fraction of an institution's total budget. In fact, these changes may benefit both institutions and their faculty members, if institutions are compelled to examine retirement policies and offer more options for retirement income. Our results give no firm assurance of what will work.

It appears, however, that carefully constructed ERIs offer the best solution for meeting the competing goals of institutional personnel policies and of faculty members who want to continue their professional affiliations, while at the same time assuaging generalized fears that changing the MRA will have dire consequences.

## References

American Association of University Professors. "Academic Retirement and Related Subjects." *AAUP Bulletin,* 1950a, *36* (1), 97-117.

American Association of University Professors. "Academic Retirement and Related Subjects: A Report on a Study Conducted by a Joint Committee of the American Association of University Professors and the Association of American Colleges." *AAUP Bulletin,* 1950b, *36* (2), 308-320.

American Association of University Professors. "Statement of Principles on Academic Retirement and Insurance Plans." *AAUP Bulletin,* 1969, *55* (3), 386-387.

Corwin, T. W., and Knepper, P. R. *Finance and Employment Implications of Raising the Mandatory Retirement Age for Faculty.* Washington, D.C.: American Council on Education, 1978.

Greenough, W. C. *College Retirement and Insurance Plans.* New York: Columbia University Press, 1948.

Greenough, W. C., and King, F. P. *Benefit Plans in American Colleges.* New York: Columbia University Press, 1969.

Hansen, W. L., and Holden, K. C. *Mandatory Retirement in Higher Education.* Unpublished report for the U.S. Department of Labor. Madison: Department of Economics, University of Wisconsin, 1981.

King, F. P., and Cook, T. J. *Benefit Plans in Higher Education.* New York: Columbia University Press, 1980.

Ladd, E. C., Jr., and Lipset, S. M. "Many Professors Would Postpone Retirement If Law Were Changed." *The Chronicle of Higher Education,* 1977, *15* (10), 7-8.

Mulanaphy, J. M. *Plan and Expectations for Retirement of TIAA-CREF Participants.* New York: Educational Research Division, TIAA, 1981.

Reimers, C. "The Timing of Retirement of American Men." Unpublished doctoral dissertation, Columbia University, 1977.

U.S. Department of Labor. *Final Report to Congress on Age Discrimination in Employment Act Studies.* Washington, D.C.: U.S. Department of Labor, 1982.

*Karen C. Holden is senior scientist, Institute for Research on Poverty and the Institute of Aging, University of Wisconsin-Madison.*

*W. Lee Hansen is professor of economics and of educational policy studies, University of Wisconsin-Madison.*

*The results of the COFHE studies on the effects of raising the mandatory retirement age from sixty-five to seventy are presented.*

# Findings from the COFHE Studies

Sarah Montgomery

This chapter summarizes the major findings of three studies conducted in 1979-80 for the Consortium on the Financing of Higher Education (COFHE), a group of thirty private colleges and universities, on the potential impact of extending the minimum age of mandatory retirement from sixty-five to seventy. COFHE institutions are all private and are principally in the northeastern United States. They are equally divided between universities and colleges, the latter of which include six women's colleges. (For various reasons, data from several of the institutions were omitted from each of the data bases; the three studies summarized here are available from COFHE, 238 Main St., Cambridge, MA 02139.)

Two sets of data on the arts and science faculties of the COFHE schools underpin these reports. One set came from institutional data for 1974-78 on all faculty members who were tenured or in tenure-track positions. Data were obtained on ages, salaries, dates of appointment and award of tenure, and the reasons for and dates of all terminations, includ-

---

The author was a member of the COFHE steering committee for these studies. The results are reported from the viewpoint of a reader, not a writer, of the studies. The emphasis and, to some extent, the interpretations of the results may not be those of the investigation.

ing retirement. The second set resulted from a mail questionnaire sent in 1979 to 1,621 eligible faculty members forty years old and older. This survey obtained information on personal characteristics, asked about attitudes toward work and retirement, and solicited reactions to several possible early-retirement plans. The response rate was 75 percent, with no difference in response rates by age or sex (Institute for Research in Social Behavior, 1980).

**The Actuarial Study: Effects on Hiring and Payroll**

Southworth and Jaqmin (1979) used the historical data on faculty flows from 1974 to 1978 to estimate retrospectively what the impact on these institutions would have been if the mandatory retirement age during those years had been seventy. Their simulations assume that all faculty members who had worked up to the previous MRA delayed retirement to age seventy, and that 1974-78 salary scales remained unchanged. The impact of the change in the MRA under these worst-case conditions was simulated under alternative assumptions about institutions' responses to the higher salary costs and to the reduced number of faculty vacancies caused by the extension of work life. (This situation is considered the worst case from the standpoint of salary costs and availability of new openings. The assumption that no deaths or disabilities occur among faculty members who extend employment to age seventy also overstates the effect of that change.)

The highest-cost scenario was one in which the number of tenure awards and new appointments remained the same as during those years. Faculty size would have increased by approximately 2.1 percent after five years, and payroll costs would have risen by approximately 2.8 percent. If the payroll budget and tenure awards had been held constant, the number of new appointments would have fallen by 13.0 percent over the five-year period, and the size of the faculty would have declined by 1.9 percent. A third simulation fixed both faculty size and the ratio of tenure awards to the number of nontenured faculty. This would have reduced new hiring by 7.0 percent over the five-year period and increased payroll costs by about 1.25 percent.

These simulations for the 1974-78 period were based on the faculty age structure actually observed in those years. In projecting the probable effect of a higher MRA after 1978, Southworth and Jaqmin (1979) recognized that natural aging alone would lead to higher payroll costs. Therefore, in simulating the effect of a higher MRA between 1979 and 1998, they distinguished the effects of natural aging and those due to an MRA of seventy by comparing simulation results with and without an extension of the MRA. In each instance, they adopted their worst-case assumptions. Further, they assumed that all new appointments were to nontenured positions, that the turnover rate of nontenured faculty was 20 percent each year, and that the tenure-expectation ratio—tenure awards as a percent of the total number of nontenured faculty reductions each year—averaged 36 percent.

This corresponds roughly to the 1974-78 COFHE experience. For example, of 2,788 active nontenured faculty members as of January 1, 1978, 19.8 percent moved out of that status during the year—7.1 percent were promoted into tenure slots, and 12.6 percent left for other reasons. About 25.0 percent of the new hires during this period were in tenured positions, but these were almost exactly matched by the number of terminations of tenured faculty members for reasons other than death, disability, or retirement. Thus, tenured new hires and separated tenured faculty could be ignored in the simulations (Southworth and Jaqmin, 1979).

In the absence of any MRA change, the over-sixty faculty group was projected to increase by more than 30 percent in the first five years because of natural aging. Holding faculty size constant, Southworth and Jaqmin estimated that payroll costs would have increased in the first five-year interval by 2 percent, because of faculty aging alone, and by almost 3 percent in the second five-year period (Table 1). The reduction in retirements would force new hires to fall by 5 percent in the first five years, but by 1994-98, as older faculty members retired, new hires would have increased by 4 percent, when compared to the late 1970s.

When the simulations were rerun to include an MRA of seventy, with

Table 1. Summary of Payroll and Hiring Projections: Assuming Constant Faculty Size[a]

|  | *After Five Years* | *After Ten Years* | *After Twenty Years* |
|---|---|---|---|
|  | *Cost Increases as a Percentage of Payroll* | | |
| Without change in MRA | 2.00 | 2.75 | 1.50 |
| Isolated impact of age-70 MRA | 1.50 | 2.00 | 2.00 |
| Total | 3.50 | 4.75 | 3.50 |
|  | *Effect on New Appointments* | | |
| Without change in MRA | −5.00 | −8.00 | +4.00 |
| Isolated impact of age-70 MRA | −9.00 | −9.00 | −7.00 |
| Total | −14.00 | −17.00 | −3.00 |

[a]The simulations were for four five-year periods: 1979-83, 1984-88, 1989-93, and 1994-1998. The end of the twenty-year period is January 1, 1999. The MRA was assumed to change to seventy at all institutions on January 1, 1979.

*Source:* Southworth and Jaqmin, 1979.

faculty size held constant, the impact remained greatest in the second five years of the simulation. But even when faculty members "matured," payroll costs rose by an additional 2 percent as a result of the extended MRA. New hiring, by contrast, although it increased at the end of the simulation period because of age-structure effects alone, suffered a net decrease because of later retirements.

When payroll costs, rather than faculty size, are held constant, the effect on new hires is even greater, since job openings are diminished both by delayed retirements and by the higher salaries paid to delayed retirees (these simulations are not shown in the table). In this case, faculty members' aging alone was projected to decrease new hiring by 16 percent in the first five-year period and by 21 percent in the second. The total faculty size is its smallest, at 4 percent below its initial size after ten years, but by the end of the twenty-year period, new hires have increased by 9 percent. Assuming an MRA of seventy, the greatest decrease in new appointments—19 percent in the first five years—occurs soon after that change, and faculty size is smallest at the end of the ten-year period. As retirements increase, however, the number of new hires is up by 1 percent in the 1994-98 period.

**Effects of a Higher MRA on Voluntary Retirement**

A second study, by Blackburn and Schiffman (1980), also used the historical data on faculty flows to separate the effects of simultaneous changes in the MRA from the age structure of the COFHE faculty cohort. This study emphasizes that if faculties are aging, the effects of a later MRA will be extended over a longer period. For example, when a faculty age structure is balanced (that is, if faculty members are distributed equally across all age groups), and if everyone reaching age sixty-five postpones retirement to age seventy, only during the first five years will there be a reduction in the number of retirements. After that period, the number of retirements in each year will be the same as before the MRA change. A younger faculty, however, will diminish the immediate effects of the change in the MRA and spread them over a longer period.

Blackburn and Schiffman began with the 1978 age structure of the COFHE faculty cohort, projected annual retirements through 1993 under then-current MRA policies, and compared these results with those assuming a change in 1982 to an MRA of seventy. Although differences in the number of retirements become quite small by 1990, even as late as 1993 there are fewer retirements with an MRA of seventy than without it.

To estimate the retirement patterns of faculty members, Blackburn and Schiffman did not make Southworth and Jaqmin's (1979) worst-case assumptions about delayed retirements. Instead, they used data on voluntary retirement at COFHE institutions that did not have special early-retirement incentives. The percentages of people retiring before age sixty-five and at ages sixty-five and sixty-six were estimated from the experience of six institutions where the MRA was between sixty-eight and seventy. The percentages of those retiring at ages sixty-seven and sixty-eight were based on the experience of two schools with an MRA of seventy. For reasons described in the Blackburn and Schiffman study, the percentage of people retiring voluntarily at age sixty-nine could not be directly determined; that rate was arbitrarily set.

The estimates imply that approximately 50 percent of faculty members will retire voluntarily before age seventy, and that there will be an average retirement age of sixty-eight and one-half with an MRA of seventy. This is more than two years later than the actual average retirement age for 1974-78, which was just over sixty-six at all COFHE schools.

Both studies (Southworth and Jaqmin, 1979; Blackburn and Schiffman, 1980) implicitly hold constant two factors thought to have large potential effects on retirement decisions: actual or expected rates of inflation, and pension plans. Although they do not attempt to model these effects, Blackburn and Schiffman note that each of the COFHE schools with early-retirement schemes had a lower average retirement age than did those with the same MRA but with no such plans. They also suggest, as a rough and upper-bound estimate based on evidence from a limited number of institutions, that when faculty members between sixty-five and seventy are paid a retirement bonus equal to approximately one-third of their salaries, about one-third of them will retire at sixty-five to sixty-seven; the effect is to reduce the average age of retirement by a year and a half. Nevertheless, it is difficult to use these historical data to estimate the effects of early-retirement schemes because of very limited experience with these plans at that time. (Many of the schools have adopted early-retirement schemes since then.)

## The Faculty Survey: Effects of Inflation and Financial Incentives

An analysis of the faculty survey data by the Institute for Research in Social Behavior (IRSB) (1980) explicitly sought information on the effects of inflation and various early-retirement incentives (ERIs) on projected retirement dates. Data were analyzed only for faculty members who could continue to work to age seventy, either because their institutions had an MRA no lower than seventy or because they were too young to be affected by the MRA of sixty-five to sixty-nine allowed during the seven-year exemption period. The retirement-age data refer not to actual retirements but rather to the age at which faculty members thought they might retire under various circumstances.

The primary question posed to the respondents was their expected retirement age. The majority of the faculty members in each age group anticipated retiring before age seventy. Even among those who were sixty-one and older, only 46 percent anticipated continuing full-time teaching until the later mandatory retirement age. The average expected retirement age for this oldest group was 68.2, which is close to the average age of 68.5 in the Blackburn and Schiffman (1980) simulation of the age-seventy MRA; in that study, however, both the percentage retiring at seventy and the percentage retiring before sixty-five are substantially higher than in the IRSB survey.

The faculty survey may have underestimated the number who would delay retirement until age seventy, if responding faculty members had not had sufficient time after the change in the law to adjust their retirement expectations to the new environment. Caution in interpreting these data is suggested on the basis of answers to the question "How much serious thought have you given to your retirement?" Among those forty to fifty-four, only 49 percent said they had given it "a great deal" or "some" consideration, compared to 71 percent of those fifty-five to sixty and 83 percent of those sixty-one and older.

The IRSB investigators hoped to learn more about the relative importance of financial considerations for a faculty member's decision about when to retire. A number of pieces of evidence in their report deal with this issue. Faculty members responded to a list of possible fears about retirement, including its effects on their physical health, professional status, and self-esteem. Among respondents fifty years or older, 60 percent said that they feared "not having enough money," while 26 percent were worried about "having to find another job to supplement [their] income." Other fears on the list were selected by fewer than 25 percent of the respondents.

Faculty members also were asked how adequate they expected their income to be one to two years after retirement and five years after retirement. Although 70 percent of those fifty-five to sixty years old and 74 percent of those sixty-one and over thought their income would be adequate in the first couple of years, only 44 percent of the younger and 38 percent of the older age group expected their income to be adequate after they had been retired five years. When all respondents fifty-five or older were divided into those who expected to retire at age seventy and those who planned to retire at age sixty-five or earlier, 83 percent of the latter group but only 63 percent of the former expected to have adequate income immediately upon retiring. Furthermore, 52 percent of the early retirees, but only 36 percent of those planning to wait until age seventy, expected adequate income after five years. The reason most frequently given for waiting until seventy to retire was the need for a full-time teaching salary.

The analysis also sought to find the best single predictor of whether a respondent would delay retirement to age seventy or retire voluntarily at an earlier time. Among those sixty-one and over, the most powerful predictor was fear of inadequate income during the first two years of retirement. Only 40 percent of those who expected their income to be adequate expected to retire as late as age seventy, while 80 percent of those not expecting adequate income planned to do so. For those who were fifty-five to sixty, the most powerful predictor concerned their feelings about the prospect of retirement, rather than about expected income. This was not surprising, because for this group, whose retirement was still years away, specific pension benefits and retirement activities were less easily defined.

Respondents were also asked explicitly about the effect of inflation on their retirement expectations. They were asked whether they would "probably decide to work longer" (1) "if inflation continues to average between 9 and 11 percent a year until the age you now expect to retire" or (2) "if inflation gets even worse and reaches 15 to 17 percent a year by the time you retire." Responses did not differ much by age; 55 percent of those fifty-five to sixty and those sixty-one and over answered the first question affirmatively, and an additional 20 percent of each group said they would work longer if inflation went to the higher rate. These answers suggest that while faculty members did consider inflation rates, they did not expect the high level of inflation (9–11 percent) to persist until and throughout their retirement.

The study also sought to discover how faculty members might respond to ERIs. Respondents were asked at what age they would retire under each of five alternative ERI options (Table 2). Two phased-retirement options and three early, "total" retirement options were presented. The phased-retirement options would both be available as early as age sixty, with full pension contributions and medical benefits continuing until retirement, but one (labeled P-1) would pay 60 percent, and the other (labeled P-2) would pay 70 percent of full-time salary for half-time teaching or research. The three early-retirement options would each become available at age sixty-two, and "all usual university courtesies" and current medical benefits would continue into retirement. Plan C-1 would provide a guaranteed retirement payment equal to 40 percent of the final year's gross salary, with the institution supplementing pension and social security, if necessary. Plan C-2 was the same as plan C-1, but with annual cost-of-living adjustments equal to those received by regular active faculty members up to the "normal" retirement age. Plan C-3 was the same as plan C-1, but with retirement payments equal to 60 percent of the final year's gross salary.

About half of those between fifty and sixty and one-third of those sixty-one and older said they would phase into retirement if they could earn 60 percent of their salaries for half-time teaching. Another 10 per-

Table 2. Responses to Proposed Early-Retirement Plans

| Retirement Option | Percent Choosing Plan | Average Reduction in Teaching Years[a] |
|---|---|---|
| *Phased Retirement* (50% teaching) | | |
| Plan P-1 (60% salary) | | |
| 50–54-year-olds | 52 | 1.25 |
| 55–60-year-olds | 49 | 1.25 |
| 61 and older | 34 | 0.6 |
| Plan P-2 (70% salary) | | |
| 50–54-year-olds | 59 | 1.8 |
| 55–60-year-olds | 54 | 1.8 |
| 61 and older | 41 | 0.8 |
| *Early-Retirement Plans* (at age 62) | | |
| Plan C-1 (40% final salary) | | |
| 50–54-year-olds | 19 | 0.4 |
| 55–60-year-olds | 16 | 0.5 |
| 61 and older | 15 | 0.4 |
| Plan C-2 (40% plus COLA) | | |
| 50–54-year-olds | 26 | 0.6 |
| 55–60-year-olds | 22 | 0.7 |
| 61 and older | 19 | 0.4 |
| Plan C-3 (60% final salary) | | |
| 50–54-year-olds | 49 | 1.4 |
| 55–60-year-olds | 40 | 1.4 |
| 61 and older | 36 | 0.9 |

*Source:* Institute for Research in Social Behavior, 1980.
[a] The first six rows have been recalculated by the author to include the effects of both earlier retirement and reduced hours.

cent in each age group said they would also be attracted by the more generous phased-retirement option. Under the less generous (60 percent) plan, the average reduction in teaching years would be 1.25 for those sixty and under and 0.6 for those sixty-one and over. If they were paid 70.0 percent of their salaries, the average reduction would be 1.8 years for the younger group and 0.8 years for the older group.

The percentage of faculty members who would change their retirement timing is never as large under the early-retirement options as under the phased-retirement schemes. (The only exception is the 34 percent among those sixty-one and older who would change their retirement age under the first phased-retirement plan, compared to the 36 percent in this age group who would change that age under plan C-3.) The reduction in teaching years under plan C-3, however, is roughly comparable to that under the more generous of the phased-retirement plans. The changes indicated under plan C-1 are startlingly large. From 15 to 19 percent of the faculty indicated they would retire earlier if guaranteed 40 percent of final gross salary. Typically, however, the COFHE institutions already replaced at least 50 percent of final-year pay upon retirement at age sixty-five, which means they would have replaced about 40 percent of final-year pay as early as age sixty-two. Thus, these responses may indicate less about the incentive power of the ERI scheme than about the respondents' lack of precise knowledge about their existing pension plans. If, in fact, faculty members underestimate the benefits available from their existing pension plans, ERIs may not change retirement ages by as much as these data suggest. By contrast, the data gathered in these surveys on expected retirement ages may overestimate the age at which faculty members will retire if, as they approach retirement, they become aware of and respond to the more-generous-than-expected pension benefits.

**Possible Effects of Uncapping**

Although these reports looked only at the impact of changing the MRA to seventy and did not address the issue of uncapping, their findings may be used to speculate on the effects of having no mandatory retirement age. For many COFHE institutions, the concern about the effects of uncapping is linked to the TIAA pensions that cover most of their faculty members. As retirement is delayed, the eventual annual annuity payment rises, for three reasons. Additional contributions will be made during the additional years of work. Even more important are interest earnings on all prior accumulations. Finally, because retirement benefits must be paid for one less year, an actuarial increase will also increase annual pension benefits. Taken together, increases in TIAA benefits as retirement is delayed provide a powerful financial incentive for some faculty members to continue working. Further, the unusually high rates of inflation at the time of the survey no doubt influenced respondents' concerns about whether retirement income would continue to be adequate over a long retirement. These fears may have affected not only the retirement expectations of those with below-average TIAA accumulations but also the expectations of those with larger accumulations.

Most older respondents to the survey deemed their current income sufficient for their consumption needs and expected their retirement income to meet those needs as well. Among respondents sixty-one and older, 78 percent said their current income allowed them to buy "almost everything" or "most of the things" they wanted, although only 51 percent said it allowed them to save a "reasonable amount" above their pension contributions. But about one-fourth of the faculty respondents (all of whom were employed) did not anticipate having adequate income immediately after retiring. Only a minority of the faculty respondents expected their income to be adequate five years after retirement. Those who expressed concern about inadequate income were more likely to say they would delay retirement until age seventy. This concern, combined with the evidence that faculty members would change their plans if confronted by higher rates of inflation, suggests that some of those who anticipate no problems in meeting consumption needs at retirement may nevertheless work longer under uncapping, in order to provide for their longer-term security. If a primary goal is to attain adequate funds for a long retirement without financial worries, only a few added years of employment may be necessary to raise pensions and savings to the level where retirees feel financially secure.

Consider, for example, a faculty member who, at age sixty-five in 1980, was eligible for a TIAA pension of $12,240 per year. (These calculations were contributed by John Briggs.) Then assume that over the twenty-year life expectancy of this individual, inflation averaged 7 percent per year. By age eighty-five, inflation would have reduced the real value of that pension, first taken at sixty-five, to only $3,164. If, however, the faculty member delayed retirement until age seventy, collecting at that time a nominal TIAA annuity of $28,160, the real value of that pension at age eighty-five would be $7,278. Further postponement of retirement to age seventy-three would provide a $44,952 nominal pension at that age, which would allow the faculty member a retirement income at eighty-five of $11,619 in base-year prices. (The total TIAA accumulation at different retirement ages is calculated with the assumption of a 5 percent annual growth of salaries and a rate return on TIAA accumulations of 12 percent. This implies a real salary decline of 2 percent a year and a real rate of return of TIAA of 5 percent. This is consistent with experience during the years of the survey and the studies.)

Other findings of the survey suggest that faculty members who earn higher salaries (and, presumably, who have greater retirement benefits) are most likely to retire later. With uncapping, this group of faculty members may postpone retirement even further. In a confidential analysis distributed only to COFHE institutions, IRSB cross-classified responses to questions about retirement plans by salary levels of the respondents. When respondents who were fifty-five to sixty were grouped into five income classes, there was a consistent positive relationship between salary levels, on the one hand, and average expected retirement ages and the proportion of each income group that would plan to work to the hypothesized MRA of seventy, on the other. Among those sixty-one and older, however, this relationship between income and expected retirement age changed somewhat, with those in the lowest and highest income groups containing the greatest proportions of those who would work until seventy. The high proportion in the low-income group no doubt reflects respondents' concern about the inadequacy of expected pensions.

Conclusions about a direct effect of income on retirement age between faculty members age fifty-five and sixty must be drawn with caution, however. In the same report, IRSB divided respondents into three "merit" classes on the basis of their answers to questions about their publications, their awards, how they would rate their performance, and how they thought their colleagues would rate their performance. There was a strong positive relationship between income and merit group. Thus, it may be that faculty members in the high-income categories anticipated later retirement, not because of greater expected earnings and pension accruals, but because of the greater job satisfaction that is associated with membership in a higher-merit and more productive group.

## Conclusion

The results of the three COFHE studies indicate that with the change in the MRA from sixty-five to seventy, more faculty members anticipated working beyond age sixty-five. This postponement would cause total payroll costs to rise, and if the total size of the faculty did not grow, the number of new hires would have to fall. On the basis of the experience of the few institutions with an MRA of seventy, the average delay in retirement was predicted to be about two years. From limited institutional experience at that time with ERIs, and from faculty members' responses to hypothetical ERIs, it appears that more generous early-retirement payments would encourage earlier retirements. Further, one group of delayed retirees includes those whose careers have been most productive.

The effects of uncapping are difficult to unravel because these studies did not directly address that question. Nevertheless, the results suggest that some faculty members will delay retirement by a few years to achieve more security, but others will delay retirement because of relatively greater success in their fields. These delays could be mitigated by ERIs, about which faculty respondents expressed great interest. ERIs that include some type of phased-retirement option promise to have the greatest influence on retirement timing.

## References

Blackburn, J. O., and Schiffman, S. *Faculty Retirement at the COFHE Institutions: An Analysis of the Impact of Age-70 Mandatory Retirement and Options for Institutional Response.* Cambridge, Mass.: Consortium on the Financing of Higher Education, 1980.
Institute for Research in Social Behavior. *Retirement Plans and Related Factors Among Faculty at COFHE Institutions.* Oakland, Calif.: Institute for Research in Social Behavior, 1980.
Southworth, J. R., and Jaqmin, R. A. *Potential Financing and Employment Impact of Age-70 Mandatory Retirement Legislation on COFHE Institutions.* London: Tillinghast, Nelson & Warren, 1979.

*Sarah Montgomery is professor of economics at Mount Holyoke College.*

*Because of the strong disincentives to work that are embedded in social security and many employee pensions, most workers will continue to retire in their early sixties despite the uncapping of the mandatory retirement age.*

# An Economywide View of Changing Mandatory Retirement Rules

*Richard V. Burkhauser, Joseph F. Quinn*

Other chapters in this volume look at the 1978 and 1986 amendments to the Age Discrimination in Employment Act with respect to the effects on institutions of higher education alone. To put that discussion in a broader context, this chapter considers the impact of increasing the minimum legal MRA on retirement patterns of older adults across the entire economy.

Simply raising or eliminating the MRA will not guarantee a dramatic change in retirement behavior. Most workers are now free to continue working past age sixty-five, but they do so in the face of sharp reductions in their net earnings. Even though firms may not lower wages explicitly, they may change overall compensation packages as workers near retirement age. Before 1978, most firms with a mandatory retirement age also offered some form of pension. The payout rules used in these pensions provide strong incentives to leave work, as do social security benefit rules.

**Actual and Planned Retirement**

In Chapters Three and Four, faculty members' expected retirement age was the variable used to evaluate the effects of the mandatory retirement age on retirement timing. Economists have been generally skeptical about using expectations as a measure of what people actually do. Data are now available, however, that link retirement plans to actual outcomes, allowing analysis of the closeness of that relationship. Anderson, Burkhauser, and Quinn (1986) used data from the Retirement History Study (RHS), a ten-year longitudinal survey (1969-1979) of people who were between fifty-eight and sixty-three when the study began. In 1969, workers had been asked when they planned to retire.

Table 1 compares expected retirement ages for male workers with the ages at which they actually retired. The bottom row shows that 24 percent retired at least one year before they had planned to in 1969, 57 percent retired within a year of the planned age, and 19 percent retired at least a year late. While the correspondence is not perfect, we found that a clear majority did retire at the planned age.

We then tried to discover why some workers missed their targets. We separate the reasons for change in retirement plans into three categories: (1) an unexpected event in one's personal life, the most obvious of which (and the one we consider) is a health problem; (2) an unexpected institutional change, the most important of which (and the one we consider for our sample period) is the substantial unexpected increase in real social security benefits in the early 1970s; and (3) the ability of workers to adjust to new or more accurate information, an ability we associate with age (as workers near the planned retirement age, they may spend more time looking into the ramifications of their decisions and change their minds, or they may be less flexible about responding to new information as the

Table 1. Retirement Behavior Relative to Retirement Plans
(Male Workers Employed in 1969)

| Age in 1969 | Earlier Than Planned (%) | About When Planned (%) | Later Than Planned (%) | N |
|---|---|---|---|---|
| 58 | 32 | 47 | 20 | 343 |
| 59 | 25 | 55 | 20 | 295 |
| 60 | 29 | 54 | 17 | 297 |
| 61 | 17 | 62 | 21 | 250 |
| 62 | 18 | 64 | 18 | 257 |
| 63 | 9 | 76 | 15 | 138 |
| 58-63 | 24 | 57 | 19 | 1,580 |

*Note:* Horizontal rows total 100 percent.
*Source:* Anderson, Burkhauser, and Quinn, 1986.

planned retirement date draws near). We used a multinomial logit estimation procedure to determine the degree to which these three phenomena affected the accuracy of planned retirement age, and we summarize our findings here.

***Health Changes.*** We expected deterioration in health to increase the probability of earlier-than-planned retirement and to decrease later-than-planned retirement. Data from the RHS allowed us to trace self-reported health from 1969 to the year of planned or actual retirement, whichever came first. We found that those who reported worsening health were more likely to retire before they had planned to and less likely to retire later.

***Changes in Social Security Benefits.*** The 1970s offered a natural experiment for examining the effects that major change in government policy can have on retirement behavior. For each year between 1959 and 1979, we estimated initial social security benefits for a median-wage male worker who would reach age sixty-five in that year. We assumed that the worker earned the median-wage income in each year of employment over his lifetime, and that his wife was the same age and received only a spouse's benefit. A worker turning sixty-five in 1959 would have received a total annual benefit of $1,886 (or $4,702, in 1979 dollars).

Benefits since 1959 increased, for two reasons. First, nominal wages rose, and this rise increased the wage base on which social security benefits are calculated. Second, and more important, Congress altered the formulas by which benefits are derived. Workers who had based their expectations of future social security benefits on the performance of the system between 1959 and 1968 were unlikely to have expected such change. Nominal benefits for a median-wage worker rose from $1,886 to $2,218 over that period; but, with adjustment for inflation, real benefits remained virtually constant. Such expectations with regard to the level of benefits over the next decade, however, would have represented a great underestimation of what was to come. Between 1968 and 1979, initial real social security benefits rose by more than 50 percent, with the great bulk of the increase coming by 1973.

We estimated the present value of social security benefits paid over the expected retired lifetime of each worker in our sample, assuming that real benefits followed the 1959–1968 pattern and remained constant up to planned retirement age. We then estimated the actual present value of those benefits at the expected retirement age that had been reported in 1969. The difference in the present discounted values approximates the increase in wealth caused by unexpected changes in social security policy. We found that the greater the percentage increase in total wealth due to this change, the more likely the worker was to retire earlier, and the less likely he was to retire later than he had planned.

***Influence of Age.*** Our work corroborates a finding by Holden and

Hansen (reported in Chapter Three of this volume) that the nearer the planned retirement age, the more accurately the worker sets that target age. (This pattern can be seen in Table 1.)

The 1983 amendments to the Social Security Act increased the normal social security retirement age from sixty-five to sixty-seven, but the increase will take place gradually, beginning at the turn of the century. One argument for phasing in this change was that it would be unfair to force workers who had made retirement plans under one set of rules to change those plans on the verge of retirement. Our research suggests that this is a legitimate concern. Workers in our sample who were in their late fifties and early sixties did appear to have firm ideas of when they would retire. (Bernheim, 1988, uses a more sophisticated model to compare expectations with actual retirement. His findings confirm that workers do have reasonable expectations of when they will retire.) Planned retirement age, in the majority of cases, was an accurate predictor of actual age of retirement. Unexpected changes in health or in government policy do alter retirement age, however. We found this to be true with the changes in social security policy, and it is also likely to be true with respect to MRA rule changes. Policy changes of this type are likely to alter behavior, with larger alterations occurring among workers who have more time to adjust.

**General Work Behavior of the Aged**

As earlier chapters show, most faculty members retire at age sixty-five or later and have done so throughout the 1970s and into the 1980s. This behavior contrasts with that of the average male worker over the period from 1950 through 1986. If one defines normal retirement age as the earliest age at which the majority of males are out of the labor force, then in 1950 it was about age sixty-nine. By 1960, it had fallen to about age sixty-five and remained there over the next decade. It fell dramatically in the 1970s and the 1980s and is now at about age sixty-two. Only 31 percent of males who were sixty-five years old in 1986 were in the labor force.

Another indication of the dramatic change in the work behavior of older men over that period is their increased acceptance of social security benefits. The percentage of eligible men who received benefits between the ages of sixty-two and sixty-four increased from 20 percent in 1961 (the first year that men were eligible) to 59 percent in 1986. Since 1976, the majority of men eligible to do so have taken their social security benefits before reaching age sixty-five. Among men between sixty-five and seventy-one, the percentage receiving benefits has increased from 44 percent in 1950 to 92 percent in 1986.

It can be seen, then, that a major difference in working in universities and colleges is that before passage of the 1978 amendments to the ADEA, most faculty members continued working until at least age sixty-five, whereas by the mid 1970s only about 50 percent of workers outside education continued working until age sixty-five. Mandatory retirement was probably a much more important mechanism for inducing exit from jobs in education than from other jobs in the economy.

Because faculty members tend to retire later, and because the mandatory retirement age has increased, the crucial question is this: Are there other effective ways of encouraging faculty members to leave their regular positions?

## Pension Rules and Retirement Decisions

In effect, most employers' pension plans lower the net wages of people who continue to work past some given age. To understand how this wage adjustment works, it is necessary to reject the traditional single-year view of pension benefits. The traditional replacement-rate measure of pensions—pension benefits in the year of retirement, versus wage earnings—is too crude a measure to pick up important multiyear features of pension plans.

To illustrate how a single-year view of pensions varies from a life-cycle view, consider two faculty members, each of whom could either earn $50,000 this year or retire immediately with a yearly pension of $20,000. Both pension plans have a replacement rate of 40 percent, but the rewards of work or retirement will vary according to how the pension plan counts continued service. Suppose, for example, that the first worker's pension benefit will remain at $20,000 in all future years, while the second worker's yearly benefit increases to $22,000 if he postpones acceptance for one year. For staying on the job, the second worker gets an additional $2,000 annual benefit, which to some degree offsets the $20,000 he passed up this year, whereas the first worker loses the entire $20,000. The first worker's pension plan effectively reduces his net reward for working from $50,000 to $30,000. Thus, it is not only the size of pension benefits but also the rules governing their payment that can affect a retirement decision. By shifting the pension plan's reward structure for continued work, an employer can effectively change the net earnings of workers without directly affecting stated wages.

## Effects of Rules on Net Wages

Pension rules that do not raise future benefits to compensate workers who remain on the job in effect penalize those who keep working. Most pension plans have this characteristic. After a worker reaches some age, a plan is not actuarially neutral; that is, its present value falls if the plan is not accepted before the worker reaches some threshold age. The change in the net present value of the pension must be added to stated wage earnings in order to determine the actual compensation for continued work.

For most workers past some age, social security retirement benefits also are not actuarially neutral. Hence, a major reason for reduced work effort at older ages is the decline in net wage earnings caused by actuarially unfair pension and social security rules. The rapid decrease in the labor-force participation rates of older men over the last two decades has not been confined solely to men in those age groups eligible for social security benefits. For instance, the participation rate of men who are sixty years old fell from 85 percent in 1968 to 69 percent in 1986. Hence, the influence of employers' pensions on early retirement must also be recognized.

Table 2 is based on a sample of full-time employed men between sixty-three and sixty-five in 1974. It shows the effects of pension and social security payout rules on wage earnings. Workers are divided into those eligible for social security benefits alone and those eligible for both social security and employers' pensions. On average, men of sixty-three and sixty-four, who are eligible only for social security, gain by delaying retirement. Men who continue to work at these ages receive future social security benefits that are more than sufficient to compensate them for postponing benefits now. For median workers, social security wealth changes add 13 percent to pretax earnings at age sixty-three and 10 percent at age sixty-four, but this pattern is reversed dramatically at age sixty-five. Because yearly social security benefits increase by only a token amount after age sixty-five, net earnings fall by 35 percent for the average worker. Note that almost three-quarters of workers who are sixty-five effectively suffer a reduction in wage earnings of 30 percent or more if they continue to work. This reduction in the net reward for working past age sixty-five is even more dramatic among those eligible for both social security and employers' pensions. For median workers, net wages are cut nearly in half. Over 90 percent of such workers suffer an effective pay cut of 30 percent or more because of payout rules. (Other recent work confirms the dramatic drop in pension wealth when retirement is postponed past even early retirement age; see Fields and Mitchell, 1984; Ippolito, 1986; Kotlikoff and Wise, 1987.)

**Disentangling the Effects**

To evaluate the effect of mandatory retirement rules on work effort, one must disentangle their effect from that of pensions and social security. Mandatory retirement rules were widespread in the early 1970s. Using data from the RHS, however, Burkhauser and Quinn (1983) found that

Table 2. Payout Changes[a]

| Size of Change[b] | Age of Employed Men |||
|---|---|---|---|
| | 63 | 64 | 65 |
| *Eligible for Social Security Only* | | | |
| Percentage Loss | | | |
| 30 or more | 0 | 6 | 74 |
| 10 to under 30 | 3 | 4 | 17 |
| Under 10 | 17 | 18 | 9 |
| Percentage Gain | | | |
| 0 to under 10 | 23 | 22 | 0 |
| 10 to under 20 | 24 | 32 | 0 |
| 20 to under 30 | 23 | 10 | 0 |
| 30 or more | 11 | 8 | 0 |
| Total Sample | 100 | 100 | 100 |
| Median Change in Present Value | +13 | +10 | −35 |
| *Eligible for Social Security and Employer Pension* | | | |
| Percentage Loss | | | |
| 30 or more | 6 | 15 | 92 |
| 10 to under 30 | 1 | 18 | 6 |
| Under 10 | 18 | 22 | 2 |
| Percentage Gain | | | |
| 0 to under 10 | 18 | 19 | 0 |
| 10 to under 20 | 34 | 22 | 0 |
| 20 to under 30 | 17 | 4 | 0 |
| 30 or more | 7 | 0 | 0 |
| Total Sample | 100 | 100 | 100 |
| Median Change in Present Value | +12 | −3 | −48 |

[a] Table shows distribution of workers by changes in present value of employers' pensions and social security, associated with an additional year of work as a percentage of annual before-tax earnings for full-time employed men sixty-three to sixty-five in 1974.
[b] Expressed as a percentage of annual before-tax earnings.
*Source:* Quinn and Burkhauser, 1983.

most of those who faced mandatory retirement rules were also eligible for pension benefits. Of men between sixty-two and sixty-four in 1973 who over the next two years reached a mandatory retirement age, 77 percent were also eligible for pension benefits at that time. Of the remaining 23 percent, 17 percent were eligible to collect pension benefits later, and only 6 percent were never eligible for benefits. In contrast, less than 50 percent of workers who had no mandatory retirement age on their current jobs were or would ever be eligible for pensions on those jobs.

Most workers with mandatory retirement ages also had pensions, but this fact requires caution in comparing the work effort of those with and without mandatory retirement ages on their jobs. When we considered the people in our sample who were sixty-two to sixty-four in 1973, and who would reach mandatory retirement age by 1975, we found that 83 percent had stopped working, whereas only 40 percent of those not so constrained had stopped by 1975. But, as Table 2 suggests, this gross comparison overstates the importance of mandatory retirement rules on work behavior. Those facing mandatory retirement were more likely also to face substantial reductions in their net wage earnings if they continued to work.

What would people facing mandatory retirement have done in the absence of that constraint? Our estimates are that 63 percent would have retired by 1975, rather than the 83 percent who actually did retire. Thus, while mandatory retirement rules may have some retirement-inducing effect, it is much less than simple comparison of the two groups would suggest. More than half of the actual difference can be explained by factors other than mandatory retirement rules.

As an additional measure of the importance of mandatory retirement rules, we took our sample of fully employed men, sixty-two to sixty-four years old in 1973, and simulated the effect that raising the mandatory retirement age to seventy would have had on their labor force participation rates in 1975. We found that fifty thousand additional men from that cohort would have been in the labor force. In other words, the participation rate of that age group would have increased by only about 2 percent and would have had an inconsequential effect on the aggregate economy.

## Conclusion

Raising the mandatory retirement age from sixty-five to seventy has had no appreciable economywide effect on the work effort of older men. The work effort of men sixty and older continued to fall during the 1980s. Uncapping of the mandatory retirement age will not by itself reverse this trend. Workers who faced mandatory retirement from their jobs were also likely to face pension payout rules that encouraged retirement.

Nevertheless, uncapping may have much more important effects in certain industries and occupations. Historically, the work effort of older people has been greater in higher education than in other industries. Mandatory retirement has been more widespread, and educators have been more likely to work until it was imposed. In addition, defined-contribution pension plans are common in higher education. Because defined-contribution plans are also likely to be actuarially neutral with regard to payout, reductions in net wages of the type discussed earlier are less likely at universities than in other settings. Thus, raising the mandatory retirement age to seventy, or eliminating it altogether, would have a much more important impact on higher education than on the economy as a whole.

Even so, the final outcome may be less dramatic than anticipated. The 1986 amendments to the ADEA required firms with pension plans to continue providing credit to those who continued working past normal retirement age, but this requirement does not preclude offering faculty members special bonuses to retire early. In the years since higher education institutions have been subject to the MRA of seventy, there has been a substantial increase in so-called faculty buyout plans. Totally uncapping the MRA would undoubtedly make such buyout plans an expensive but regular feature of our industry.

## References

Anderson, K. H., Burkhauser, R. V., and Quinn, J. F. "Do Retirement Dreams Come True? The Effect of Unexpected Events on Retirement Age." *Industrial and Labor Relations Review*, 1986, *39* (4), 518-526.
Bernheim, B. D. "Social Security Benefits: An Empirical Study of Expectations and Realizations." In R. Ricardo-Campbell and E. Lazear (eds.), *Issues in Contemporary Retirement.* Stanford, Calif.: Hoover Institution, 1988.
Burkhauser, R. V., and Quinn, J. F. "Is Mandatory Retirement Overrated? Evidence from the 1970s." *Journal of Human Resources*, 1983, *18* (3), 337-358.
Fields, G. S., and Mitchell, O. S. *Retirement, Pensions, and Social Security.* Cambridge, Mass.: MIT Press, 1984.
Ippolito, R. A. *Pensions, Economics, and Public Policy.* Homewood, Ill.: Dow Jones-Irwin, 1986.
Kotlikoff, L. J., and Wise, D. A. "Pension Backloading, Wage Taxes, and Work Disincentives." National Bureau of Economic Research Working Paper no. 2463. Cambridge, Mass.: National Bureau of Economic Research, 1987.
Quinn, J. F., and Burkhauser, R. V. "Influencing Retirement Behavior: A Key Issue for Social Security." *Journal of Policy Analysis and Management*, 1983, *3* (1), 1-13.

*Richard V. Burkhauser is professor of economics and senior fellow, Institute for Public Policy at Vanderbilt University.*

*Joseph F. Quinn is professor of economics at Boston College.*

*Uncapping the mandatory retirement age is unlikely to alter retirement age by much, but it will lead to substantially higher pensions for faculty members who continue to work.*

# Eliminating Mandatory Retirement: Effects on Retirement Age

*Karen C. Holden, W. Lee Hansen*

Elimination of a mandatory retirement age, as a means of compelling retirement by faculty members after 1993, has forced institutions to examine the purposes, structures, and age-related characteristics of their pension policies. Even without uncapping, recent changes in the tax law, legislated increases in the age when unreduced social security benefits will be paid in the future, social pressure for flexible retirement options, and, not least of all, the earlier shift in the MRA to age seventy would in any case have led to such a reexamination. Nevertheless, eliminating this link between age and retirement raises questions about what *normal retirement age* and *delayed retirement* mean and about how to set retirement income objectives.

Early in the history of pension plans, institutions of higher education typically recognized no difference in these two concepts of retirement age; pensions were expected to be paid at the age when faculty members faced mandatory retirement. In recent years, however, the MRAs at many colleges and universities diverged from and were later than the normal retirement age (that is, the earliest age when full pension benefits would be available). This divergence was sharpest in public institutions covered by state plans, where the normal retirement age was more often earlier or defined jointly by years of service and age (Johnson, 1987). In 1980, 73 percent of all institutions of higher education set sixty-five as their normal age of retirement (representing 97 percent of the private institutions but only 62 percent of the public institutions), even though only one-third of all institutions then had an MRA of sixty-five.

Thus, before passage of the 1984 amendments to the ADEA, retirement was effectively bracketed by the age when full retirement benefits first became available and the age of mandatory retirement. Earlier retirement was discouraged by the smaller benefits based on lower levels of earnings and service and because of actuarial reductions in those benefits. Conversely, because delayed retirement led to higher benefits, it was argued that a mandated age of retirement was necessary to ensure that faculty would not work well past the normal retirement age. While the 1978 amendments to the ADEA, which raised the minimum allowed age of mandatory retirement to seventy, increased the potential age range of institutionally allowed retirements, they did not destroy the notion that limits on that range were important.

Without an MRA, the structure of pension plans, as well as the incentives they provide to continued employment, become of greater consequence. This chapter examines these issues. We begin by reviewing the ground rules that have prevailed, offer some limited evidence about the effects of uncapping on average retirement age, discuss how pension benefits change as retirement is delayed, and offer some conclusions about the effects of uncapping.

**Ground Rules**

Through a series of statements by the Joint Committee on Academic Retirement and Insurance Plans of the American Association of University Professors (AAUP) and the Association of American Colleges (AAC), higher education has periodically examined and given general guidance on the level of pension benefits that should be provided through institutional retirement programs.

> Normal retirement . . . is a term employed in retirement planning to designate an age for setting retirement income objectives and contribution rates. The stated normal retirement age may be earlier than or may coincide with the mandatory retirement age. . . . The availability of an adequate retirement income at the normal retirement age can give individuals an economically viable choice of retiring before the mandatory age. . . . The recommended objective for those retiring at the normal retirement age who have participated in the plan for at least thirty-five years is an after-tax income [including any payments available through the federal

social security system] equivalent in purchasing power to approximately two-thirds of the yearly disposable salary (after taxes and other mandatory deductions) during the last few years of employment [American Association of University Professors, 1969, p. 386].

All references to a mandatory retirement age have been eliminated in the 1988 revision of the AAUP/AAC joint statement. The statement now recommends a normal retirement age within the age range of sixty-two to seventy-two and suggests that retirement income adequacy be measured against an employee's last few years of full-time employment (American Association of University Professors, 1988). These changes are attempts to cope with the uncapping of the mandatory retirement age. Nevertheless, how institutions should treat individuals who wish to delay retirement is not addressed, and recommendations for normal, early, and phased retirement remain unchanged. Thus, the AAUP/AAC 1988 statement fails to address an important question facing institutions: In the absence of any MRA, beginning in 1994, should other incentives be developed to encourage the timely retirement of faculty members?

**Retirement Timing with Uncapping**

Little information is available to predict how retirement patterns will change with uncapping. Some institutions have recently abolished mandatory retirement, largely in response to changes in state legislation, but there has been no systematic effort to collect data on their experience before and after that change. Because a few institutions in our survey (described more fully in Chapter Three) had no MRA, we can gain some understanding of the effects of uncapping.

Recall (from Chapter Three) that institutions with an MRA of sixty-five reported higher retirement rates by their tenured faculty members between sixty-five and sixty-nine than did institutions with an MRA of seventy. We concluded that while most institutions with an MRA of sixty-five allowed faculty members to extend employment beyond age sixty-five, the process of having to request and receive approval for such extensions appeared to reduce the number of years that faculty continued teaching beyond the MRA. Our prediction that a lifting of the mandatory retirement age from sixty-five to seventy would lead to later retirements— by slightly more than a year, on average, but by more at private institutions—is borne out in a 1987 study by the Consortium on the Financing of Higher Education (COFHE). Among the thirty-six institutions surveyed where the mandatory retirement age was raised from sixty-five to seventy, the average age at retirement rose from 64.6 in academic year 1982 to 66.0 in academic year 1986. At a subset of twenty-three COFHE institutions—primarily private colleges and universities—the average age increased from 64.7 to 66.3 years. These increases imply, and our estimates confirm, that even when the MRA increased to seventy, only a minority of faculty members waited until age seventy to retire—28 percent of retirees in all thirty-six institutions, and 31 percent in the COFHE colleges and universities.

What will happen after 1993, when institutions will be prevented from maintaining any MRA? In our earlier work (see Chapter Three), we argued that an MRA of sixty-five discouraged extensions for the full five-year period to age seventy and led to higher retirement rates from age sixty-five to seventy than with an MRA of seventy. Likewise, we expect that an MRA of seventy would discourage continuation of faculty members beyond age seventy and would cause retirement rates before age seventy to be higher than if there were no MRA. Thus, we proceed by hypothesizing that faculty members at four-year colleges and universities that change from an MRA of seventy to no MRA will behave as faculty members did who were already at institutions without an MRA in 1980. (For this comparison, we excluded two-year colleges, which were most likely to report no mandatory retirement age. The somewhat different mission and administrative structure of these institutions may make their experience incomparable to what is likely to happen in four-year colleges and universities.) The evidence shows, however, that the percentage of faculty members who retired at seventy and above was approximately the same at these two types of institutions. Moreover, the percentage of faculty members retiring at age sixty-five to sixty-nine at institutions with no MRA was actually higher than at institutions with an MRA of seventy. This evidence suggests either that uncapping the MRA is likely to have little or no effect on the average age of retirement or that institutions can adopt programs to mitigate that effect.

Several caveats are in order. First, our results are based on the limited number of institutions in our survey with no MRAs, and these institutions may not be typical of the wide range of institutions affected by uncapping. Second, the evidence is based on data from the late 1970s and the early 1980s, when high rates of inflation may have altered long-term retirement patterns; hence, it may not be applicable to the late 1980s and the early 1990s. Third, even in institutions that had no mandatory retirement policies, retirement rates for 1980 may not reflect the long-term results of uncapping. Finally, retirement rates may not yet have changed in institutions where uncapping occurred right after the 1978 ADEA amendments. Such changes are likely to occur as later retirement in higher education becomes both more prevalent and more acceptable, in the absence of any mandatory retirement age.

At the same time, this evidence suggests that the major transformation in retirement policies in higher education has already taken place. The switch to an MRA of seventy has already exerted its full effect on retirement patterns; the further shift to uncapping will have little or no influence on the retirement timing of faculty members.

**Pension Benefits and the Mandatory Retirement Age**

We argued in Chapter Three, as did Burkhauser and Quinn in Chapter Five, that the actual age of retirement may be influenced not only by an MRA but also by the provisions of pension plans. At the minimum, the availability of pension benefits permits faculty members to quit paid employment. More important, the level of income replacement, and the changes in pension income that result from continuing to work, are generally thought to play an important role in retirement timing. The concern in higher education is that without a mandatory retirement age, pension plans in which replacement rates rise with age and pension benefits increase will cause faculty members to postpone retirement. Using the admittedly limited data available from our survey, we want to examine how pension income changes as retirement is delayed.

In doing this, it is important to distinguish between the two types of pension plans in higher education: defined-contribution plans and defined-benefit plans. In defined-contribution plans, benefits are based on contributions from individuals and from the institution. Typically, the contribution rate is expressed as a percentage of current salary, although in many institutions this percentage may vary by salary level, rank, and service. Regular contributions accumulate in each individual's name. At retirement, the accumulated contributions plus dividends determine the size of the annuity that can be paid out over the individual's remaining lifetime (and that of his or her survivor, if some form of survivor's benefit is chosen). TIAA-CREF plans are defined-contribution plans. In our sample, such plans covered 78 percent of all full-time faculty members in private institutions and 21 percent of those in public institutions.

In a defined-benefit plan, the benefits are determined by formula. In higher education, the formula typically multiplies a constant—ranging in public institutions in our earlier sample from 1.4 to 2.0—by years of service and by final average salary (typically over the last three to five years). (This is a somewhat narrower range than the current one of 1.1 to 2.5; some plans were not included in our earlier sample, and some states have improved benefits since then.) Even when some combination of employees' and employers' contributions is made, these do not enter directly into the determination of benefit levels. Defined-benefit plans are the general rule in the public sector and hence cover the majority of faculty members in public colleges and universities (King and Cook, 1980). Nevertheless, because many public institutions offer TIAA as the primary plan, only 55 percent of all faculty members in 1980 were in institutions that offered state plans as the primary option.

The American Association of University Professors (1988) statement reflects an implicit assumption that the replacement level of salary by retirement income is the major way in which pensions influence retirement behavior. Did academic institutions achieve the goal of replacing two-thirds of preretirement salary levels? How does that replacement rate change with postponed retirement?

To calculate the annual annuity for which a person would be eligible at age sixty-five under each of the public and private institutional plans in our sample, we constructed a wage profile for an "average" full-time faculty member, who started teaching at age thirty-two, with a beginning salary of $3,200, and in 1980 at age sixty-four earned $33,150 as a full professor. (This salary profile was estimated from historical AAUP salary data and takes changes in rank into account. Our hypothetical employee is a reasonable approximation of the long-term employee to whom AAUP/AAC recommendations are directed.) Because we assume a single salary profile, our results are not influenced by career or institutional changes that may differ among individuals. Benefits available at age sixty-five to this long-term employee, under each of the various plans, were estimated from plan descriptions. We know from descriptions provided by each institution what benefits a retiring faculty member would receive at age sixty-five, given a particular salary profile and service history. The 1980 benefit formula was used in estimating defined-benefit plan payments, and the 1980 TIAA contribution schedule was used to estimate the annual payments in those plans. We assumed that all TIAA-CREF contributions reported by faculty members were held by TIAA. The value of the TIAA accumulation was calculated, assuming a long-term interest factor of 6.0 percent and a 3.5 percent administrative expense charge on new contributions, and the annuity payable from the TIAA accumulation at age sixty-five was derived from TIAA tables for 1980.

On average, this hypothetical faculty member would receive a pretax pension benefit equal in public plans to 60 percent of average salary over the last three years and in TIAA plans to 63 percent of the three-year salary average. This replacement rate would be lowered by taxes but increased by social security, by any supplemental annuities, and by the savings of the individual. In comparisons of state plans, however, considerable variation occurs in the nominal value of the annuity for which a faculty member with the assumed salary schedule would be eligible at age sixty-five. The most generous state plan pays more than twice that of the least generous (replacing 85 percent versus only 34 percent of the three-year final average salary). Similar variation in TIAA plans is also observed, with combined employers' and employees' contributions in TIAA-covered institutions ranging from 5 percent to 20 percent in our sample of institutions. Thus, some institutions fall far short of the replacement goal recommended by the AAUP/AAC committee.

As Burkhauser and Quinn asked in Chapter Five, what happens to replacement rates if retirement is postponed for a year? The answer, of course, depends on what happens that year to salary levels, which will affect the size of both the denominator and the numerator, and (under a defined-contribution plan) on what happens to contribution levels. An absolute freeze on retirement benefits can take place only in a defined-benefit plan in which no salary and service credits are permitted past some age or level. If both are credited, an additional year of higher salaries will raise the final salary averages, and an additional year of earnings will increase the service factor. In a defined-contribution plan, even if contributions cease, continued dividends on the accumulation to date, combined with the actuarial adjustment, will raise benefit levels. In theory, then, it is possible (if legally permitted) for defined-benefit plans to freeze benefits, but this cannot be done in defined-contribution plans. In fact, defined-benefit plans may no longer freeze benefits at a fixed age, even though they may set maximum service credits (see Chapter One). Even at the time of our survey, however, when the freezing of benefits was permitted at age sixty-five, the majority of defined-benefit plans did not do so.

Consider, then, what happens in state (defined-benefit) plans when retirement is postponed from sixty-five to sixty-six. In our sample, we based pension amounts on the salary and service profiles already outlined. We also assumed that the individual's salary increased by 8 percent in that year, and that an additional year of service was credited. In this case, the annual pension benefit received one year later would be higher (by 11 percent, in our example), but the increase in the replacement rate would be modest (from 60 percent to 62 percent). Surprisingly, TIAA plans show similar percentage increases in nominal benefits, with the result that replacement rates rise from 63 percent to 65 percent. In defined-benefit plans, this increase comes through the recalculation of benefits with a year of higher earnings and an additional year of service. In TIAA plans, by contrast, higher benefits result as total accumulations increase from additional dividends, additional contributions paid out of one more year's salary, and the actuarial adjustment made for the delay in receiving benefits. Apparently, and despite very different plan structures, annual benefits from defined-benefit and defined-contribution plans increase comparably, on the average, as retirement is postponed.

**Pensions and Postponement of Retirement**

There is some fear that this rise in annual benefits, together with the small change in replacement rates, will encourage individuals to postpone retirement because they would be better off financially. This fear, however, fails to take account of the value of the benefits postponed for one year and the extent to which they are compensated for through higher payments over an individual's remaining lifetime. Only if the present value of additional benefits in the next and all other years of retirement is more than equal to those forgone benefits would an individual add to his or her pension wealth by postponing retirement. This is not true in all plans, however, and it is less likely to happen when high rates of inflation erode the real value of future benefits. Even in TIAA, where actuarial adjustments are made, the present value of postponed benefits may be reduced by inflation and by the preference of individuals for current over future income.

We used data from our survey to estimate what would happen to pension wealth if our hypothetical faculty member postponed retirement from sixty-five to sixty-six. To estimate the wealth value of defined-benefit payments, we used an adjusted Individual Annuity Mortality Table (Cherry, 1971), which conformed to TIAA participants' mortality experience. (It is interesting to note that, at age sixty-five, the expectation of life for faculty members is about eighteen years, four years more than for the total U.S. population.) A real discount rate of 5 percent and a long-term inflation rate of 5 percent per annum were assumed. In addition, the TIAA pension was conservatively assumed to be paid at the guaranteed amount throughout the individual's lifetime, and the annual amount paid by a state pension was adjusted to inflation only if CPI adjustments (or partial adjustments) were automatic in that plan.

If annual pension benefits are discounted at 5.0 percent, the present value of postponed benefits increases in absolute size, but by only a modest 1.4 percent. This modest change would be offset by the decline in social security wealth of 3.7 percent when benefits are delayed from sixty-five to sixty-six. For some plans, the increase in pension benefits with a 5.0 percent discount rate is higher by as much as 6.0 percent, but for others there is a decline as small as 3.0 percent. If higher discount rates are used (as would have been appropriate at the time of our survey, when inflation was higher than it is now), faculty members on the average would lose in both types of plans if they postponed their retirement benefits, and they would have even bigger losses if social security benefits were considered.

To the extent that pension wealth does not change substantially with an additional year of work, the incentive to continue working for that additional year is diminished. Thus, it may be that once faculty members achieve targeted levels of pension income, pension structure does not further delay retirement. Such factors as salary, professional involvement, collegial relations, teaching environment, and personal preference for additional leisure time become important. Indeed, our analysis (Hansen and Holden, 1981) indicates that, among older faculty members (sixty-two to sixty-four), pensions do not significantly influence retirement expectations. As argued in Chapter Three, the factors that do influence this group appear to be institutional involvement, salary levels, research output, and the mandatory retirement age. Thus, it appears that MRA does matter, partly because pension incentives are now roughly neutral for retirement-age choices.

## Conclusions

Our data do not permit us to draw firm conclusions about the effects of uncapping on the timing of faculty members' retirement. Retirement rates in the late 1970s—for faculty members sixty-five and older at institutions with an MRA of seventy and at those with no MRA—imply that the shift to uncapping is unlikely to exert any substantial effect on the pattern of retirement timing. This does not mean that the shift from an MRA of sixty-five to seventy had no effect; indeed, the effect predicted from our 1980 study is consistent with COFHE data on what has happened since then. Still, caution is required, because the relatively few institutions without an MRA in 1980 may be quite different from the full range of institutions that will not be subject to any MRA in the 1990s. Thus, we cannot be as certain about the effects of uncapping as we were about the effects of raising the MRA.

Concern has been expressed that the increase in pension benefits from delayed retirement is larger under TIAA than under state pension plans, and TIAA-covered faculty members are therefore more likely to postpone retirement than are those in public institutions. The argument is that, during the additional year of work, total TIAA accumulations continue to earn dividends and raise the total value of the lifetime annuity. In addition, the benefit amount will be increased by actuarial adjustment for receipt at a later age. Nevertheless, we found that the percentage change in annuity levels for a hypothetical faculty member is no greater than the change in public pension plans that continue to credit additional years of service and higher earnings. This conclusion is consistent with data from our faculty sample on total TIAA-CREF accumulations and on salary and work histories that we used to construct their individually anticipated annuities. Thus, unless participants in public and TIAA plans discount benefits differently, the percentage change in their wealth from postponing benefits is identical.

A different reward for the postponement of benefits will result only if institutions are willing and legally able to alter the rate at which contributions are paid to TIAA, as well as the crediting of service and earnings to public plans as faculty members pass normal retirement age. Through the cessation of service and earnings credits after some age, benefits under defined-benefit plans can be frozen. This cannot be done under TIAA, but dividends on current accumulations continue, and actuarial contributions are made. Defined-benefit plans cannot end service and earnings credits at some particular age; they can do so only after some number of service years. Doing so, however, discourages faculty members with long years of service from continuing to work, and these may not be the individuals whose retirement is preferred.

Our results are subject to one important qualification: By using the hypothetical salary profile we outlined, we may have overestimated TIAA benefit levels. First, in many TIAA plans, institutional contributions to individual retirement accounts cease at some age. Second, over the years, colleges and universities have increased the total required contribution; hence, our example will overestimate contributions for earlier years. We may also overestimate actual pensions from state plans to the extent that we fail to account for the effects of early job mobility on total years covered by a single plan. From faculty members' responses to our questions about their TIAA-CREF accumulations and about their years of service and current salaries when they were covered by state plans, we find this to be the case. Projected benefits are about 81 percent and 86 percent of the estimated amount for the hypothetical long-term service worker in TIAA and public plans, respectively. The net result, however, is that, across faculty members in the two types of plans, the average absolute value and replacement rates of salary are almost identical. As in our hypothetical example, the average benefit will (on the average) increase by the same percent in the two plans; only if the crediting of salary increases and service is restricted will the benefit increase be smaller in public than in TIAA plans. This similarity in benefit levels suggests that while faculty members in TIAA plans may be disadvantaged by low employer contributions during their early teaching years, the pension amount is no lower than that for faculty members in public plans who moved around during their early years.

If replacement rates are used as a barometer of financial security in retirement, faculty members in some institutions enter retirement with fewer financial resources than are recommended by the AAUP/AAC standards. Replacement rates, however, vary across both types of plans. For individuals with less generous pensions, an MRA was probably a severe constraint on their ability to achieve a more secure retirement, but this was true in both defined-contribution and defined-benefit plans. Uncapping will increase retirement-age options and thus retirement security. From our analysis, however, it does not appear that for individuals who continue full-time employment beyond age sixty-two, pension benefits play a major role in determining when they will retire. Other factors, including institutional affiliation and professional income from other sources, must play a more important role.

Faculty members may indeed be responsive to nonneutral pension incentives, whether introduced as reforms to basic pension plans or as supplements that increase the pension wealth of those who retire (relative to the wealth of those who delay retirement). Under the 1986 amendments to the ADEA, the cessation of pension contributions at a set age may now be more difficult, but the combination of phased retirement options (as outlined in Chapter Three) and pension supplements may help lower retirement age or at least prevent it from rising.

The prospect of uncapping does not appear as bleak now as it did in the late 1970s and the early 1980s. There is little solid evidence that faculty members wish to work beyond age seventy. Nevertheless, long-term experience with a higher MRA or with no MRA comes primarily from a few four-year colleges and public universities and thus may predict little about the overall effects of uncapping on private institutions. Because institutions are now limited in how they can restructure pensions legally to accomplish age-related objectives, higher education must vigorously pursue studies of retirement-age behavior under uncapping. Information from such studies will allow the restructuring of pensions and other fringe benefits to better meet income and retirement objectives in the new environment.

## References

American Association of University Professors. "Statement of Principles on Academic Retirement and Insurance Plans." *AAUP Bulletin*, 1969, *55* (3), 386-387.

American Association of University Professors. "Statement of Principles on Academic Retirement and Insurance Plans." *AAUP Bulletin*, 1988, *74* (1), 37-38.

Cherry, H. "The 1971 Individual Annuity Mortality Table." *Transactions: Society of Actuaries*, 1971, *23* (11), 498.

Consortium on the Financing of Higher Education. *Early Retirement Programs for Faculty: A Survey of Thirty-Six Institutions.* Cambridge, Mass.: Consortium on the Financing of Higher Education, 1987.

Hansen, W. L., and Holden, K. C. *Mandatory Retirement in Higher Education.* Unpublished report for the U.S. Department of Labor. Madison: Department of Economics, University of Wisconsin, 1981.

Johnson, B. *Public Retirement Systems: Summaries of Public Retirement Plans Covering Colleges and Universities-1987.* New York: Teachers Insurance and Annuity Association, 1987.

King, F. P., and Cook, T. J. *Benefit Plans in Higher Education.* New York: Columbia University Press, 1980.


*Karen C. Holden is senior scientist, Institute for Research on Poverty and the Institute on Aging, University of Wisconsin-Madison.*

*W. Lee Hansen is professor of economics and of education policy studies, University of Wisconsin-Madison.*

*Tenure arrangements are long-term contracts. If their duration is clear, they will protect academic freedom, provide institutions with the flexibility needed to meet changing circumstances, and comply with age-discrimination laws.*

# Implications of the 1986 ADEA Amendments for Tenure and Retirement

*Oscar M. Ruebhausen*

Tension is growing between the legitimate concerns of our society about age discrimination and the important educational policies reflected in the use of age as a criterion for either the termination of faculty tenure contracts or faculty retirement at institutions of higher education. (For a fuller discussion of age as a criterion, see Ruebhausen, 1986.) The challenge to higher education is to operate a retirement program that fits the tenure system, serves the educational objectives of colleges and universities, conforms with the age-discrimination laws, and maintains the self-esteem of retirees and utilizes their talents while being sufficiently flexible to accommodate the special and changing needs of the individual and the institution.

The existing tension increased with the enactment of the Age Discrimination in Employment Amendments of 1986 (the 1986 amendments), which amended the Age Discrimination in Employment Act (ADEA) of

---

This chapter is a revised version of Ruebhausen (1988). The author thanks the National Association of College and University Attorneys for permission to reprint material that first appeared in the association's journal.

1967. Before the 1986 amendments, the protections of the ADEA were limited to employees between the ages of forty and seventy. The 1986 amendments eliminated (uncapped) the upper age limit, so that the protections of the ADEA now extend to employees over the age of forty. The 1986 amendments also contain a special rule for tenured faculty members.

**The Tenure Arrangement**

To understand the implications of the 1986 amendments for tenured faculty, one must first understand the tenure arrangement. Tenure is a contract between the employing institution and the tenured faculty member. This view of tenure may startle those in academia who consider tenure a status, not a contractual arrangement. Viewing tenure as a contract, however, is crucial to analyzing the impact of the age-discrimination laws on tenure and retirement.

The tenure arrangement involves an extraordinary commitment by a college or a university. It is a commitment of continuing employment for a long term, typically until normal retirement age. Tenure provides genuine job security, subject only to the financial exigency of the institution or to cause given by the faculty member. This commitment contains an understanding that continued employment will not depend on a regular review of job performance. Promotions or increases in salaries may depend on job performance, but continued employment will not (see AAUP/AAC Commission on Academic Tenure, 1973).

There is a powerful internal coherence to a contract in which the institution forgoes performance appraisal as a condition for the continuation of faculty members in their jobs (until the agreed termination date), while the faculty member forgoes performance appraisal as the criterion for the expiration of the tenure contract on the agreed date.

In the abstract, it is hard to believe that any employer would make an employment commitment for as long as thirty-five years. Indeed, such commitments are not normally made either in the public or the private sector. There are rare exceptions, however, such as the lifetime commitment made to some judges in order to secure the freedom and objectivity of judgment that is deemed worth the potential cost in efficiency, a trade-off comparable to tenure in higher education.

This extraordinary tenure commitment binds the college or university. It is a contract enforceable by the faculty member. The contract also binds the faculty member. Normally, however, no written document labeled a tenure contract sets forth all or even most of the conditions of tenured employment, nor is any such document formally signed by the institution and the faculty member. The absence of a formal document may encourage the perception that no contract exists. A contract, however, does exist, although no formal document is needed to create it.

*Duration.* The absence of a written document can create trouble, especially if it leaves uncertain or ambiguous any major provisions of the tenure arrangement. The contract provision that should be the least ambiguous, in the context of the age-discrimination laws, is the duration of the tenure arrangement.

In the absence of a written agreement, how can one tell whether a tenure contract is a contract for life or a contract for a fixed term ending on an agreed date? The answer lies in the relevant written materials and in the unwritten understanding of the administrators and the faculty member at any particular institution. This answer can be established only by a thorough, time-consuming review of behavioral patterns and of all the pertinent written materials. These materials include personnel manuals, faculty handbooks, faculty resolutions, legislation adopted by an academic senate, institutional policy statements, trustee resolutions, by-laws, rulings of academic committees, collective bargaining agreements, retirement programs, letters of faculty appointment or promotion, and acceptances by tenured faculty members of their tenure appointment. Prevailing custom also plays a role. Even with such a review, ambiguities will probably remain. For example, some institutions conventionally refer to a tenure appointment as an appointment without term.

*Appointment Without Term.* The phrase *appointment without term* could have several meanings. It could mean that there is in fact no agreed term. If so, then the institution could terminate the arrangement at will, as it already is terminable at will by the faculty member. While that is one possible interpretation, it is clearly not what the phrase is intended to mean.

The phrase could also mean that the term of appointment is unlimited. If so, does this mean a contract for life? In practice, this is neither the way the tenure contract appears to have been administered nor the basis on which retirement benefits have been developed. In any event, a life contract is also a contract for an agreed term, even though its duration is uncertain.

The phrase *appointment without term* probably is used simply as a form of shorthand, to distinguish tenure appointments from short-term appointments of one, two, or five years. In many institutions, such short-term appointments exist alongside the tenure system and are universally referred to as term appointments. The phrase *appointment without term* illustrates the troublesome ambiguities that institutions and their faculty members face in determining the agreed provisions of existing tenure contracts.

All institutions and faculty members must, as an essential first step, identify and clearly make explicit the terms of their tenure contracts that are now in effect. If ambiguities exist, then it becomes important to clarify the principal rights and duties of the institution and the faculty members under the tenure arrangement. In the age-discrimination context, the duration of the tenure contract must be fixed beyond a doubt. Only with knowledge of the tenure contract's duration will it be possible to assess the impact of the 1986 amendments.

*Is Termination of Tenure Retirement?* One more point must be emphasized about the tenure arrangement: There is a clear distinction between termination of the tenure contract and actual retirement. The expiration of the tenure contract and retirement from further employment are two quite different events. These two events may or may not occur simultaneously.

This distinction between retirement and the termination of the tenure contract is often ignored, partly because the two events very frequently occur together. Each addresses a somewhat different aspect of employment termination—the tenure contract deals with the end of a special employment relationship, retirement with the end of all further employment. Finally, confusion arises because the word *retirement* is often used loosely to describe a wide variety of events. Its primary meaning in the context of employment laws—namely, the cessation of paid employment—consequently tends to be obscured. The expiration of the tenure arrangement may properly be called a retirement from the tenured position, but such retirement need not be retirement from continuing full-time or part-time paid employment by the same or another employer. Lack of precision in the use of the word *retirement* can be troublesome.

Accordingly, it is important that the tenure contract be clear on the question of retirement. There should be no ambiguity about whether the expiration date for tenure is also intended to be the date for retirement from the employing institution, or about whether the termination of the tenure contract is without prejudice to a subsequent contract of employment for a new term of years. In practice, many institutions follow the expiration of tenure contracts with renewable contracts for terms of one or more years.

Unfortunately, academic intention with respect to whether the expiration of the tenure contract is to be followed by retirement or by a new contract for a short term (often renewable) is usually revealed by the custom and behavior of the institution and its faculty, rather than by any explicit provision in the governing documents. It is also unfortunate that these subsequent short-term contracts are often not clearly perceived as posttenure contracts but are misperceived as postretirement contracts.

Nevertheless, it is the hypothesis of this chapter that institutions typically intend the tenure contract to be an employment contract for a term that will expire after an extended period of years. The normal expiration date of the contract is fixed by reference to chronological age and may (but need not) be followed by retirement.

If this hypothesis—that tenure is for an agreed term that expires on an agreed date (and not of unlimited duration)—were incorrect, then the academic practice of retirement at age sixty-five (and, more recently, at age seventy) could have been a breach by the institution of the tenure contract. The present author knows of no cases, however, in which a breach-of-contract contention has been made in court.

### The ADEA Amendments

Under the original ADEA, enacted in 1967, it was unlawful to refuse to hire, and unlawful to discharge, an individual because of age, but it was not unlawful to refuse to hire, or to discharge, an individual because of reasonable factors other than age. Until January 1, 1987, these ADEA provisions applied only to employees between the ages of forty and seventy. In short, the ADEA itself used age as a criterion of social policy—that before age forty and after age seventy, it was acceptable to refuse to hire, and acceptable to discharge, solely on the basis of age.

The 1986 amendments changed this social policy by removing the upper age specification for protected employees. It is no longer acceptable policy to refuse to hire, or to discharge, solely by reason of age at any time after age forty. Although the policy is clear, it will rarely be equally clear whether any particular refusal to hire, or any particular discharge, is based on age rather than on other reasonable factors. A determination of that issue may demand difficult proof, and the outcome will depend on all the facts of each case. Nothing in the ADEA or in the 1986 amendments prohibits either agreements to terminate employment or agreements to retire at an agreed date.

***The Special Rule for Tenured Faculty Members.*** The 1986 amendments established a temporary "special rule," which is sometimes described as exempting tenured faculty members over seventy from the age-discrimination prohibitions, but that is not how the legal language reads. Indeed, nothing in the amended ADEA prohibits "compulsory" retirement of any tenured faculty member who has reached the age of seventy. Several provisions of this special rule deserve particular attention. Notice that the exemption applies only to "compulsory" retirement. Thus, while it exempts compulsory retirement of tenured faculty members, it does not exempt tenured faculty members whose retirement is not compulsory. Put another way, the special rule does not exempt tenured faculty members *as a class;* it exempts only a limited type of retirement.

This particular language is important for two reasons. First, the statutory language tends to confirm that the intent of the ADEA is to apply only to "involuntary" or "compulsory" retirement—namely, discharge or dismissal, rather than contractual or agreed termination. Second, the exemption extends only to retirement, and not to hiring. Therefore, the

1986 amendments preserve the unlawfulness of refusing to hire faculty members, whether or not they have been previously tenured, if refusal to hire is based on age and not on other reasonable factors.

Accordingly, since January 1, 1987, in considering the employment or reemployment of faculty members after age forty, the college or university must base any refusal to hire on factors other than age. Under existing policies, this requirement may trouble some institutions.

*Posttenure Employment.* Any policy against rehiring faculty members after the expiration of their tenure contracts is suspect unless it is clearly based on factors other than age. Institutions that typically do not rehire faculty members after the expiration of their tenured employment contracts face a current and immediate problem. The problem will arise whenever the policy against rehiring appears to have been followed, regardless of institutional or departmental need for a faculty member, and whether or not the faculty member's desire and fitness to continue are beyond doubt.

There is a potential trap here for the unwary dean or administrator. This trap can be escaped through a specific agreement to retire. (Such agreements are involved in the familiar practice of providing, on a nondiscriminatory basis, incentives to retire early—the so-called buyouts.) A temporary escape route may also be found if courts broadly interpret "compulsory" retirement (intended to be exempted under the special rule) to include arbitrary refusal to rehire immediately after a tenure contract expires. Certainly, an inflexible policy of refusing to discuss or consider a reemployment arrangement could be viewed as transforming the expiration of the tenure contract simultaneously into a compulsory retirement. As such, a court might find the policy exempt under the new special rule. No academic institution is likely to adopt knowingly so rigid and risky a policy, however, since more reasonable alternatives are available. In any event, individuals currently involved in faculty hiring should be carefully instructed about the narrow scope of the new language and the potential illegality of refusing to rehire after the age of seventy, solely because of age.

*Special Rule Confined to Unlimited Tenure.* In addition to the limited exemption for "compulsory" retirement in the 1986 amendments, a second provision in the new special rule for tenured faculty members also deserves attention—namely, the limitation of the exemption to employees who are serving under contracts of unlimited tenure. The exemption accordingly applies only to the "compulsory" retirement of faculty members who have unlimited tenure. Nevertheless, the meaning of the phrase *unlimited tenure* is far from clear in the context of the amendments.

The Senate Special Committee on Aging did not explain its intent in limiting the rule to those employees having unlimited tenure, nor was its intent clarified or commented on during House or Senate discussions.

Does *unlimited tenure,* as used in the special rule, simply mean tenure? Does it mean tenure for a life term, a term without a fixed duration, or something else? Whatever the phrase *unlimited tenure* means, to know whether the new exemption applies means that the duration of the tenure contract must be clear. If a tenure contract is expressly stated to be for an unlimited term, then the exemption should apply, and "compulsory" termination of the unlimited tenure contract by reason of age, at age seventy or later, would be permissible under the ADEA (for seven years). Nevertheless, an institution might then face a dilemma, since its compulsory termination of unlimited tenure would seem to breach the explicitly unlimited tenure set forth in the contract.

By contrast, however, if tenure is a contractual arrangement between an institution and a faculty member for a fixed term that expires on an agreed date, then the exemption would seem not to apply, nor would an exemption be needed for such a contractual arrangement. Indeed, in such a case, it would be counterproductive for an institution to act as if the exemption applied. After all, if an institution's tenure contract has an agreed expiration date, then when the contract expires, the end of employment is consensual; it does not represent age discrimination. "Compulsory" retirement, however, is termination of employment without consent. It is the equivalent of dismissal or discharge with no intention to reemploy, and it is unlawful after age forty if it occurs solely on the basis of age.

Accordingly, the ADEA does not prohibit the carrying out of an agreement for the expiration of tenured employment on a fixed date. Similarly, the use of chronological age to fix an agreed date, either for retirement or for the termination of tenured employment, is not the arbitrary action forbidden by law. Those who used the term *unlimited tenure* may have misunderstood what colleges and universities, and their faculties, are doing pursuant to the tenure system. The amendments' drafters may have believed that colleges and universities were discharging tenured faculty members because of age, before the end of their contractual agreements. This is not what was or is happening, and any such misunderstanding must be corrected.

***Duration of Special Rule.*** The special rule for tenured faculty members will, by express provision, last only seven years unless Congress takes further action. In addition, Congress has mandated a study during the next five years to analyze possible consequences of eliminating mandatory retirement from institutions of higher education. This study, to be conducted under the supervision of the National Academy of Sciences, could serve as a unique and objective forum to discuss such issues as the nature of the tenure contract, the distinction between retirement and expiration of tenure, and the status of the faculty employee upon the expiration of the tenure contract and the extent of the institution's obligation (if any) to rehire. Still other topics of discussion might include the distinction between discharge and expiration of tenure, the importance of the tenure arrangement, the need for a tenured term of a fixed duration, and the use of chronological age as an agreed criterion for the expiration of the tenure contract. The study will provide institutions of higher education and their faculties an opportunity to explain carefully the nature and role of the tenure contract in higher education. The study also presents an opportunity to draft and justify proposed new findings or legislation for Congress with respect to tenure and retirement in academia.

**Courses of Action**

Two principal courses of action are indicated for academic institutions and their faculties, one external and the other internal. The external course is to assist the National Academy of Sciences and its research panelists to fulfill the leadership role Congress has placed upon them.

The internal course may be more complicated. For example, the duration of tenure contracts should be clearly stated, both in current and in future contracts. This is not a trivial requirement. If the duration of the tenure agreement is fixed, as a matter of educational and institutional policy, for a genuine educational purpose and is stated expressly in the tenure contract, then the expiration of tenured employment should not fall within the ADEA prohibitions.

How should this second course be undertaken? No single answer can be provided for all colleges and universities and their faculties. What must be done at any particular institution depends on a close understanding of its relationships, expectations, governing rules, and practices. Moreover, any clarification should be based firmly on educational policy and should not be a subterfuge for age discrimination.

Some possible patterns of response can be identified. In rare cases, no response will be needed. At a minimum, most institutions will probably want to include in all future letters of tenure appointment (initial as well as confirmation letters) an express understanding that the tenure appointment contract will end on a specified date, subject to early termination for adequate cause or institutional financial exigency. As a matter of sound practice, an institution should obtain written acceptance of tenure contracts from faculty members. Even such modest steps can be considered only with faculty members' approval: Unilateral administrative action could be perceived to threaten the essential collegial relationship between faculties and their institutions.

Further steps may be required. At some institutions, for example, it may be necessary to add clarifying statements to faculty handbooks or to governing academic rules. Any such additions must be made only after full compliance with the regular processes and procedures for such matters, including facultywide approval. In addition to clarifying the duration of tenure contracts, institutions may need to make clear whether retirement is to occur on the date when a tenured employment contract ends or whether a new employment contract may be negotiated.

Normally, when tenured faculty members cease to be employees of their colleges or universities upon the expiration of their tenure contracts, they have no automatic right to reemployment by their institutions. In some cases, reemployment is contrary to institutional practice, and such practice is accepted by faculty members. Often, however, expiration of a contract does not preclude further employment. In either situation, the contractual intention ought to be made clear. If age is used as a criterion for the termination of a tenure contract, there may be some advantage in making explicit that age is so used only for that purpose, and not for retirement.

If it is possible to continue employment beyond the end of the tenure contract, then a new contract between the faculty member and the institution must set forth the terms of the new arrangement. In this new contract, both the faculty member and the institution will be able to balance their existing needs and objectives. That balancing process involves several considerations, including the career plans and abilities of the faculty member, departmental and institutional needs, the availability and qualifications of other potential candidates to meet those needs, the continuing relevance of the faculty member's field, the currency of the faculty member's knowledge and scholarship, and of course the availability of funds. In short, rehiring after the termination of tenure calls for a fresh analysis of how best to conduct the institution's educational mission under the existing circumstances and the available alternatives. Similarly, faculty members will analyze their own objectives and available career choices.

Obviously, there is a vast difference between clarifying tenure contracts for newly tenured faculty members and clarifying existing tenure arrangements. Clarifying existing tenure contracts can be a difficult task for institutions, but in view of the broad general understanding of the tenure arrangement that now exists throughout academia, it does not seem impossible. If the task does prove too difficult, any problems should be persuasively conveyed both to the National Academy of Sciences and to Congress. An ultimate solution, for example, could be a statutory ADEA exemption for tenure contracts entered into before, say, January 1, 1991.

Institutions and their faculties might also reconsider the long-standing practice of terminating tenure contracts at a specified chronological age. This use of chronological age as the agreed criterion for the end of the tenure contract must withstand the charge of age discrimination, no matter how firmly rooted it is in educational policy or how useful it is in educational planning. Even though the charge can be rebutted successfully, it may be prudent in the future to use a different criterion if one can be effectively substituted. A new criterion could be a calendar date fixed by reference to departmental plans. Another possible but less attractive criterion is quality of performance. Functionally, a most appropriate criterion for the end of the tenure contract would be the date when a faculty member first becomes eligible for full benefits under relevant public and private pension programs. Academic freedom would thus be achieved, first through job security and then through pension security, in a direct sequence.

Another suggestion has considerable appeal: that tenure contracts be revised to express their duration in terms of a fixed number of years—say, twenty, thirty, or thirty-five (a number sufficient to protect academic freedom). Modestly differing salary levels could be fixed for different terms. The fixed term of years need not be identical for all faculty members at a particular institution. Contract duration could vary according to departmental needs and planning.

Nevertheless, institutions must carefully avoid any impression that faculty members with one term of employment are any more or less worthy than others who have different contract terms. This problem can be alleviated if faculty members personally make the choice. For example, the institution could give the individual faculty member the option of either a fixed term of years or chronological age as the criterion for termination of employment. Alternatively, the institution could allow faculty members to select as the termination any date—say, any July 1—between twenty and thirty-five years after the signing of the initial tenure contract. Other options are also possible.

Thus, at the time of the initial tenure appointment, a faculty member could choose among several different terms of employment, terms long enough to ensure academic freedom. Such a choice would also make faculty members active participants in selecting contract durations that would reflect their own desires. The choice would also enable the institution to plan and keep a balance between the continuity and the renewal it deems essential to meet its educational responsibilities. The importance of faculty choice is underscored by the fact that it may be a key to whether the ADEA applies. The more voluntary the ultimate termination of tenure appears, the less legally suspect it becomes.

Faculty mobility is highly valued by colleges and universities and by their faculties. Faculty members who move in midcareer need to negotiate a new term of employment. Of course, new tenure arrangements can be negotiated on an ad hoc basis, or the parties can accept whatever remains of a tenured term at a previous institution. Whatever the form of adjustment, the new institution's tenured term of employment should appropriately reflect the faculty member's prior professional activity.

## Conclusion

Introducing more flexibility into the fixed dates now used to terminate tenure seems consistent with academic freedom and with the mission of higher education. Such flexibility not only is reasonable but also tends to allay any suspicion that the fixed dates used to terminate tenure are merely a subterfuge for age discrimination, rather than an expression of educational policy. If greater flexibility in choice is found to be incompatible with educational policy, however, then the reasons for incompatibility must be marshaled persuasively and fully presented to the National Academy of Sciences and to Congress.

The challenge confronting higher education today is to formulate a policy for the termination of tenure that can satisfy a number of competing needs and goals. The policy must encourage both continuity and change. In addition to providing job security, the policy should preserve sufficient accountability to maximize individual growth and productivity. The policy must also provide a basis for institutional and faculty planning, with some sense of ensuring the future (notwithstanding all the inherent uncertainties of life). Moreover, the policy must be compatible with the age-discrimination laws and must serve the educational mission of colleges and universities. Further, the policy must harmonize with a retirement program that offers the retiree an adequate pension, affordable health care, and a continuing sense of self-esteem. The policy must especially be flexible enough to accommodate the dynamic need of academic institutions and their faculties for intellectual renewal. This is a daunting challenge, but surely not an impossible one.

## References

AAUP/AAC Commission on Academic Tenure. *Faculty Tenure: A Report and Recommendations.* San Francisco: Jossey-Bass, 1973.

Ruebhausen, O. M. "Age as a Criterion for the Retirement of Tenured Faculty." *The Record of the Association of the Bar of the City of New York*, 1986, *41* (16), 16-49.

Ruebhausen, O. M. "The Age Discrimination in Employment Act Amendments of 1986: Implications for Tenure and Retirement." *Journal of College and University Law*, 1988, *14* (2), 561-574.

*Oscar M. Ruebhausen is retired presiding partner of Debevoise and Plimpton, New York City, and was chair of the Commission on College Retirement from 1984 to 1987.*

*To advocate the replacement of traditional tenure arrangements by fixed-term contracts is a misreading of the ADEA amendments. More important, it may threaten academic freedom.*

# Tenure After the ADEA Amendments: A Different View

*Matthew W. Finkin*

Oscar M. Ruebhausen argues in Chapter Seven that either the ADEA, as amended in 1986, should be read to allow tenure to terminate at a certain age or date, or the abolition of tenure (as we know it) should be considered. I do not believe that such a reading of the ADEA is tenable, nor do I believe that considering the abolition of tenure is required.

Why would tenure be affected at all by the abolition of mandatory retirement (uncapping)? It has been estimated that the change in the legal minimum MRA, from sixty-five to seventy, increased payroll costs by an average of 2 percent to 3 percent, with a consequent decline in new hires (see Chapters Three and Four, this volume), and it is unlikely that uncapping will have a larger effect. The hiring decline, however, results directly from the budgetary impact of delayed retirement and the assumption of fixed budget size. Costs of this magnitude (and more) have been imposed on institutions of higher education at other times—for example,

---

This chapter is a revised version of Finkin (1988). The author thanks the National Association of College and University Attorneys for permission to reprint material that first appeared in the association's journal.

by the ravages of inflation, the quadrupling of oil prices, and compliance with other federal laws (Van Alstyne and Coldren, 1976)—without anyone's serious suggestion that tenure be abandoned.

To be sure, a more intimate connection does exist between uncapping and tenure than between tenure and the simple imposition of an additional budgetary constraint. A mandatory retirement policy can be thought of as a humane or civilized way for an institution to treat the "worn-out or inefficient" (Pritchett, 1916), after years of institutional service; that is, it is possible for an institution to carry the obsolescent or somnolent (but not incompetent) faculty member along for a period of years, so long as the prospect of a definite date of separation looms ever on the horizon and ever closer. Uncapping raises the prospect of carrying an uncertain but probably small number of unwanted faculty for an unpredictable period of time—that is, until death or voluntary retirement, or until evidence of decreasing capacity overcomes administrative and faculty reluctance to pursue an involuntary separation.

The reason for this prospect lies in the content of the tenure obligation. Tenure means that a dismissal during the term of service can be effected only upon a showing of incompetence or inability to perform, tested before a faculty hearing tribunal, through procedures akin to a trial and with the burden of proof resting on the administration (American Association of University Professors, 1984b). Because tenure requires such a showing, it is legally as well as politically difficult to dismiss a tenured professor. Academic freedom can be safeguarded only by the assurance that the ground for termination is valid and demonstrable (Machlup, 1969; Van Alstyne, 1971), even when incapacity is asserted.

Accordingly, much of Ruebhausen's discussion about uncapping and tenure relies on the assumption that if mandatory retirement is abolished, institutions will need to search for means to terminate "the worn-out or inefficient"—or to achieve greater flexibility—without the intramural procedural requirements that attend a dismissal during a faculty member's term of service.

In this chapter, the assumption of an easier means of disposing of faculty members is addressed first in the context of an overview of the ADEA. The next section addresses the effects of the ADEA and its 1986 amendments on the tenure contract. Finally, alternatives to tenure, including Ruebhausen's proposal for a long-term contract, are assessed.

**The ADEA in Outline**

The ADEA contains two prohibitions of relevance here. It is unlawful for an employer to dismiss or otherwise discriminate against any one individual with respect to compensation or terms, conditions, and privileges of employment, solely because of age. It is also unlawful for an employer to use age as a criterion for classifying employees in any way that deprives or tends to deprive them of employment opportunities or otherwise affect their status as employees because of age. The protected age bracket begins at forty. Under the 1986 amendment, it has no cap, or upper age limit.

There are three defenses of relevance to the actions that are prohibited by the ADEA. First, the employer is permitted to discharge for good cause, although the ADEA does not require an intramural hearing (as is required by tenure) in order to assert this defense. Second, the employer is permitted to act on the basis of reasonable factors other than age. Finally, it is lawful to observe the terms of a bona fide seniority system or benefit plan when this is not a subterfuge to evade the purposes ADEA.

These prohibitions are modeled on Title VII of the Civil Rights Act of 1964, which deals with discrimination on the grounds of race, sex, religion, or national origin; thus, not surprisingly, the courts have tended to look to the law developed under Title VII as a starting place for analysis under the ADEA. Under Title VII there are, generally speaking, two approaches to proving a violation in the absence of unequivocal evidence of prohibited action. A plaintiff may establish a "prima facie" case of individual disparate treatment by showing that he or she was in the protected class, was performing satisfactorily, and was discharged, and that his or her duties were assigned to a nonminority employee or that the position was held open. (In reduction-in-force cases, the last requirement obviously is modified.) This proof creates a rebuttable inference that a prohibited consideration explains the decision. The burden then shifts to the employer to articulate a legitimate, nondiscriminatory reason for the action. If the employer does so, the plaintiff may nevertheless dispel that explanation by a showing of pretext—for example, that the reason given was not actually applied, or that a pattern of discrimination by the employer exists and places the articulated reason in doubt.

This disparate-treatment approach contrasts with the theory of disparate impact: An employer's policy, neutral on its face and not intended to discriminate, may impose an impermissibly disproportionate burden on the protected class. Once that showing is made, the employer must demonstrate that the policy is nevertheless justified by business necessity. If the employer can make such a showing, the plaintiff may still prevail, if it can be shown that the proffered business reason is pretextual—for example, that the same business purpose could be served by other means having a less drastic impact on the protected class.

The U.S. Supreme Court has not yet addressed whether the disparate-impact theory applies under the ADEA, although three courts of appeals have applied it (one in a case of faculty retention in higher education), nor has the Supreme Court resolved the differences among several of the circuit courts on the application of the disparate-treatment standard. The leading view at the moment, with respect to the ADEA, asserts that a prima facie case is made if the plaintiff can show that he or she is a member of the protected class, was performing satisfactorily, and was discharged and his or her duties were assigned to someone substantially younger (Player, 1983).

To be sure, the question of adequate performance may be the pivotal issue. The plaintiff, however, need not negate the employer's defense in order to make a prima facie case. The weight of authority, according to Player (1983), is that "proof that *up to the point of discharge* the plaintiff was doing satisfactory work establishes that the plaintiff was 'qualified' " (p. 646; emphasis in original). Indeed, the plaintiff's very longevity may establish qualification, shifting the burden of proving good cause, or a reasonable factor other than age, to the employer. Further, in discharge cases, it is not always obvious that a younger person has assumed the plaintiff's duties. Nevertheless, evidence that the discharge started a chain of events "that ultimately created a vacancy filled by a younger employee" (Player, 1983, p. 648) may suffice.

Aspects of the ADEA other than burdens of proof must also be considered. Unlike Title VII, the ADEA provides for a jury trial. Like Title VII, the ADEA provides for attorneys' fees, should the plaintiff prevail against the employer; but unlike Title VII, the ADEA doubles the amount of actual damages (for example, lost income and benefits) on a judicial determination of willfulness. The Supreme Court has held that willfulness, for these purposes, is knowledge that the course of action was impermissible under the ADEA or reckless disregard of whether the action was prohibited (*Trans World Airlines* v. *Thurston*, 1985).

Although some courts show greater deference to employers' subjective evaluations under the ADEA than under Title VII (and even under Title VII the courts have proved highly deferential to institutional judgments about faculty members in higher education), a faculty member with decades of institutional service will probably be able to establish a prima facie case of age discrimination sufficient to compel the employer to produce evidence to justify the termination.

Even a tenured faculty member dismissed in accordance with academic due process for incompetence, neglect of duty, or incapacity to perform may sue under the ADEA, but the record and report of the intramural proceeding would most likely be admissible in the federal case as relevant to the "good cause" defense. It seems rather unlikely that a dismissal so effected—especially upon the recommendation of a faculty hearing committee, assuming that its composition reflects no age bias—would be upset by a federal court, absent extraordinarily strong evidence of pretext. In fact, the very rigor of the internal proceeding required for a dismissal under the tenure system, the fact that it is like a trial, the deference given to collegial judgment, and, consequently, the unlikelihood of the plaintiff's prevailing in the suit should tend to deter litigation.

Nevertheless, alternatives to tenure that involve periodic reevaluation would not reduce the prospect of litigation. In contrast to a discrete dismissal for cause, which is particular to the record in the case, the results of systems of periodic evaluation necessarily lend themselves to comparison (see *Zahorik v. Cornell University*, 1984). Strong evidence of a violation of the ADEA would thus arise from the institutional administration's failure to adequately explain why, under a system of periodic renewal or review, a younger faculty member was retained while an older faculty member in the discipline, with no worse an evaluation, was terminated. In other words, the adoption of intramural devices for terminating older faculty members that seem easier than a hearing for a cause may simply shift adjudication from an intramural to an extramural forum, making the process much more highly structured, more time-consuming, and more expensive. With this statutory outline as background, we may proceed to assess Ruebhausen's proposals.

**Tenure as Terminable at a Certain Age**

Ruebhausen advances two arguments. The first points out, rightly, that a faculty member who is accorded tenure enjoys a contractual right to serve until the age of retirement, unless he or she is terminated earlier for a justifiable reason, such as incompetence or medical incapacity. Ruebhausen concludes that tenure, as an agreement that terminates at a fixed date, is wholly unaffected by the ADEA, for termination is the product of voluntary agreement, not of compulsion; and, as Ruebhausen rightly observes, voluntary retirement is not prohibited by the ADEA.

By focusing on tenure as an individual contract, however, Ruebhausen ignores the source of the contract right. He makes it seem as if the candidate for tenure bargains with the university over what tenure means. But tenure is awarded according to institutional rules and policies, not according to bargaining over what the term *tenure* means (Finkin, 1980). Further, it is institutional policy, incorporated into the individual contract, that dictates the termination of tenure at a certain age. The professor has no choice in the matter other than to accept or reject the tenured position, subject to that condition.

In effect (although he eschews the term), Ruebhausen argues that the individual may waive rights under the ADEA as a condition of continued employment. It is most unlikely, however, that the courts would accept a prospective waiver of rights under the ADEA, any more than under Title VII (see *Alexander v. Garner-Denver Co.*, 1974). A university could not, for example, justify its policy of not promoting women to full professorships by conditioning its offers of tenured associate professorships upon female faculty members' agreement to future nonpromotion. If a knowing and voluntary making of such a contract were a defense, then in institutions where employers and employees have roughly equal bargaining power in establishing retirement rules, a provision for mandatory retirement would be insulated from attack, thereby rendering the ADEA meaningless. By such reasoning, for example, mandatory retirement provisions in collective bargaining agreements would bring unionized employers out from under the statutory proscription. This would negate the legislation's express purpose to regulate employment policies of the unionized and nonunionized alike.

Ruebhausen's second argument is more subtle. He focuses on the section of the ADEA that forbids employers to fail or refuse to hire or discharge individuals because of age. He points out, rightly, that a university could not refuse to hire or, more important, refuse to rehire on grounds of age. From this he concludes that tenure, as a contract that expires at a set age, is unaffected by the 1986 amendments, so long as the university is prepared either to rehire the detenured or to proffer legitimate non-age-related reasons for its refusal to rehire; that is, the evaporation of the tenure commitment is unaffected by the ADEA inasmuch as the detenured professor is neither being discharged nor denied rehiring on grounds of age.

The difficulty with this approach lies in other portions of the ADEA—namely, the two prohibitions discussed in the first paragraph of this chapter's outline of the ADEA. A policy that deprives professors over seventy of rights or privileges they enjoyed before reaching that age—for example, the right not to be terminated except for good cause, to be determined through an intramural hearing—would seem to fall afoul of the first prohibition, and most likely the second as well.

In sum, the uncapping of the ADEA means that tenure continues for those who formerly would have been mandatorily retired. It is that consequence to which the larger debate must be directed.

**Alternatives to Tenure**

The proposal that has the greatest appeal to Ruebhausen is for contracts of long but fixed duration in lieu of tenure. Before we assess it, however, we should evaluate other alternatives, in order to put that proposal in context. Moreover, the attractiveness of any alternative has to be measured both by its conformity to law and by its compatibility with the academic enterprise.

*Abrogation of Existing Tenure Commitments.* It could be argued that, in view of the change in law, existing tenure commitments could and should be abrogated. The abrogation of tenure would present a significant constitutional issue in the public sector and a significant contractual issue in the private sector. The abrogation of tenure in the public sector could be challenged as impermissibly impairing the obligations of a contract. The U.S. Supreme Court, in its revivification of the contract clause in 1977, made plain that the state, in abrogating contracts made with it, should be granted a lesser degree of judicial deference than when it acts to impair private contracts to achieve some public purpose (*United States Trust Co. v. New Jersey,* 1977).

What, from the standpoint of the state, could necessitate such drastic action? The state would have to argue that the change in federal law imposes difficulties in removing senior faculty. But in so doing, it would effectively reiterate the arguments made to and rejected by Congress in support of exempting tenured professors from uncapping. Congress, in providing only a seven-year exemption for tenured professors, tacitly rejected the claim of undue burden by higher education. Indeed, in sustaining against constitutional challenge the application of the ADEA to state and local government, the U.S. Supreme Court confronted the claim that the abrogation of mandatory retirement below the statutory age directly impaired the state's ability to perform its traditional governmental functions. The court rejected the argument, noting that the ADEA merely required the state "to achieve its goals in a more individualized and careful manner" than it would through involuntary retirement (*EEOC v. Wyoming,* 1983). While uncapping does not preclude dismissal for incompetence or incapacity, subject to academic due process, abolition of tenure to facilitate the removal of older faculty members would be patently contrary to the larger legislative purpose.

Institutions in the private sector might argue contractual impossibility—that is, when the law changes so as to render performance of a contract impossible, the nonperforming party is discharged of its contractual obligations. In this instance, the argument would be that the promise of tenure was conditioned expressly by its termination upon the professor's reaching a fixed age. Since the ADEA abrogates the latter condition, the institution should be excused from continuing its tenure obligation.

There are two weaknesses to that argument, one historical and the other doctrinal. Metzger (1973) points out that higher education has been characterized throughout its history by some sort of tenure system. Appointments of a "continuing" character, not subject to periodic renewal but without a mandatory age of termination, were not uncommon at the turn of the century, when the Carnegie Foundation established and administered the first inter-institutional system of faculty pensions. Even at that time, when eligibility for a Carnegie pension was set at age sixty-five, the average age of retirement for Carnegie pensioners was closer to sixty-nine; the president of the foundation found it regrettable that any "arbitrary limit [should be] set upon the active work of a teacher" (Pritchett, 1916). In fact, what was an ideal retirement policy was debated well into the late 1940s (Greenough, 1948). Thus, the historical link between tenure and mandatory retirement is not quite so tight as the contractual-impossibility argument presupposes.

More important, as a legal matter, the contractual doctrine of supervening impossibility does not apply to changes in law that make the performance of a contract more difficult, expensive, or burdensome, but not impossible (*Lloyd* v. *Murphy*, 1944). Continuing to employ those who formerly would have been superannuated, unless cause or incapacity is proved in an intramural hearing, may well be costly and burdensome, but the added burden will probably not suffice to absolve the institution of its existing obligations.

**Prospective Adoption of Short-Term Contracts.** There is no legal impediment to institutions' adopting term appointments in lieu of tenure, although the benefit of such a system would not be realized for another generation. Most commonly discussed is the substitution of periodic or rolling appointments for tenure—for example, renewable appointments of three or five years' duration.

How would such a system fare under the ADEA? To be sure, the system itself would treat the old and young alike—each group would have to stand for periodic review. But any decision adverse to a member of the protected class (meaning any faculty member over the age of forty) could be challenged under the theory of disparate treatment. Presumably, the institution could articulate legitimate, nondiscriminatory grounds for the nonrenewal, which would then have to be attacked as pretext. Thus, the case would rest largely on the plaintiff's proof concerning such matters as procedural irregularity or laxity in the nonrenewal process, comparison of his or her record with those of younger members of the department whose contracts were renewed, or statistical evidence that older members of the protected class were disproportionately subject to nonrenewal.

This system would make it easier to terminate faculty than under a system of tenure, inasmuch as the entire faculty, in essence, would be on probation, and cause for a negative decision would not have to be demonstrated intramurally. Precisely that feature, however, renders the idea antithetical to the academic enterprise. First, even sympathetic commentators have serious reservations about the practicability of such devices. The process "consumes a great deal of time, engages a good many people, and generates a substantial volume of material" (Chait and Ford, 1982). Second, because judgments are necessarily made for the short term and lack the long-term commitment of tenure, adverse decisions may be less likely than they are now, especially over time. Available (if slender) empirical evidence suggests that such systems apparently function as systems of de facto tenure. It is difficult not to renew the contract of an amiable (if unexciting) colleague who has, say, twenty years or more of service. It is likely that individuals ejected by such a system would be either those dismissable anyway under the tenure system or the disliked and highly controversial. Consequently, a system of perpetual probation inevitably would have a chilling effect on academic freedom and creativity.

*Periodic Posttenure Evaluation.* One idea, which has been discussed without connection to uncapping but will surely be debated more frequently as a result of uncapping, is the rigorous periodic evaluation of tenured faculty members. Under such a system, one or more negative evaluations might trigger more intense scrutiny, the imposition of some sanction, or dismissal.

The ADEA-related consequences of such a system are identical to the consequences of any other system of periodic review, save that any involuntary termination effected for good cause, as demonstrated in an intramural hearing, would be much more likely to withstand judicial scrutiny. In such a case, the evidence accumulated in the periodic reevaluation process (students' testimony, reviews by external referees of published work, and the like) would be relevant to the incumbent's fitness or competence, to be decided in a hearing. But a negative evaluation that has resulted from the evaluation process could not itself be evidence of unfitness; otherwise, receipt of a negative evaluation would be a self-defining condition for dismissal, and the hearing would be a meaningless formality. Such a system of posttenure review, whatever its survivability under the ADEA, would in effect make a negative evaluation a cause for dismissal. Thus, it would substitute periodic evaluation for a dismissal hearing, and it would be indistinguishable from the abolition of tenure and the adoption of a system of periodic appointments.

Is the system of posttenure review compatible with the award of tenure? Proponents of posttenure review argue that there is no inconsistency between tenure and "rigorous evaluation"; "meritocracy," they claim, "based on meticulous examination of a professor's work is at the core of academic tenure" (Chait and Ford, 1982). Nevertheless, this observation is accurate only with respect to judgments made in regard to the acquisition of tenure. Once it has been given, tenure shifts the presumption of competence to the professor. A rigorous system of periodic review would reduce the strength of that presumption (just as the neologism *posttenure review* connotes a diminution in the importance of the tenure decision).

To be sure, evaluation takes place throughout a professional career—for promotions, grants, awards, research or sabbatical leaves, and merit salary increases, to name a few instances. No one has asserted that evaluation for these and similar purposes erodes tenure. But what differs in schemes of posttenure review is that the periodic reevaluation takes place for the purpose of identifying likely candidates for dismissal, as a kind of academic search-and-destroy mission. It is perhaps for this reason that Ruebhausen observes, if only in passing, that such a scheme of periodic evaluation is precluded by the idea of tenure.

Whether a system of posttenure review could legally be applied to currently tenured faculty members hinges on the purpose and precise content of the system and the responsiveness of the courts to considerations of the kind just outlined. Two general lines of authority address the limits that tenure imposes on an institution's unilateral ability to alter significant incidents of personnel policy. The first would allow institutions to apply a change in policy retroactively so long as the modification were uniformly applied and "reasonable" (*Rehor* v. *Case Western Reserve University*, 1975). The second would rely more heavily on the norms and expectations of the academic profession as to whether the modification alters a substantial incident of tenure. (*Drans* v. *Providence College*, 1978). Under the first approach, a court might find periodic reevaluation a reasonable means of ensuring the continued performance of tenured faculty members. Under the second, the lack of widespread acceptance of the idea and the general recognition of the threat that such systems pose to academic freedom might prove legally persuasive (American Association of University Professors, 1983).

Wholly apart from legal considerations, however, systems of posttenure evaluation are subject to much the same criticism as systems of perpetual probation. To be truly rigorous, such a system must require every tenured professor to be evaluated by colleagues and outside referees and subjected to additional administrative review every five years or so. Even if the work load is staggered, as it must be for convenience, faculties and administrations would bear the burden of making tenure-like judgments of 20 percent of their tenured colleagues every year. Putting aside the intramural political consequences of such a scheme, a burden of this kind seems wholly disproportionate to the need to identify those who should be encouraged to retire voluntarily or against whom dismissal proceedings should be brought. Moreover, even if such a system is not intended to harass, it will inevitably be perceived as doing so (Perry, 1983). As a result, it will necessarily be seen as a threat to robust disciplinary, institutional, and collegial discourse, and, therefore, to academic freedom.

**Long-Term Contracts of Employment**

In response to the tightening academic labor market (and without consideration of federal antidiscrimination law), Cartter (1974) suggested a single contract of, for example, twenty years, to be awarded to faculty members after their successful completion of a probationary period. This would offer them an incentive for sustaining scholarly expertise and performance, as well as provide academic institutions with a way to retire older, nonproductive faculty members gracefully. Ruebhausen makes a similar proposal. This idea requires examination from both the legal and the academic perspective.

*Long-Term Contracts and the ADEA.* Under such a scheme, the individual, after the expiration of the long appointment, would be precluded from further appointment, would stand for periodic renewal, or would stand for only one renewal. Under periodic renewal, the current system of academic appointment (probation followed by either nonrenewal or the award of tenure) would be replaced by a three-part process: probation, a single if lengthy contract, and annual or other periodic renewals. Single renewal would also entail a three-part process: probation, a lengthy contract, and renewal (which would be, if granted, tantamount to the current concept of tenure).

The validity of preclusion from reappointment hinges on the acceptance of Ruebhausen's argument: that it would be analogous to a voluntary early-retirement scheme. As I argued earlier, I do not believe that this position can be squared with the ADEA.

Under periodic or single renewal, the institution would have the option to rehire or not at the expiration of the contract. By declining to rehire, the institution would risk being challenged under the disparate-treatment theory of discrimination, and Ruebhausen is sensitive to this issue. Even if discrete decisions not to rehire would survive scrutiny, however, it remains to be seen whether the system as a whole would survive challenge on a theory of systematic disparate treatment (or, if applicable, of disparate impact).

Even if the probationary period were lengthened to adjust for favorable market conditions, a twenty- or twenty-five-year contract most probably would be awarded, on average, to persons between six and ten years after completion of their terminal degrees. Thus, faculty members given long-term appointments would probably be in their mid thirties; consequently, the long-term contracts would expire when they were in their mid fifties (for twenty-year appointments) or early sixties (for twenty-five-year appointments). As a result, the institution might well be required to defend a policy of late-career breaks in contractual relations. To do so, the institution would have to argue that the need to ensure conformity with institutional expectations requires allowing nonrenewal at that point, without the procedural guarantees that attend a termination during the period of appointment.

It may well be that under the ADEA, as under Title VII, the courts will require the showing of necessity to be fairly rigorous; that is, the policy may have to be justified by "compelling need," not by convenience (*Leftwich* v. *Harris-Stowe State College*, 1983). But the argument for a late-career break in contractual relations, in contradistinction to a dismissal, would necessarily be predicated—as Cartter's proposal makes clear—on the widespread assumption "in academic circles that there is a relationship between the age of a faculty member and ability to produce instruction and research" (Radner and Kuh, 1977). In other words, a serious argument could be made that the policy would rest on an age stereotype that Congress tacitly rejected by declining to adopt a blanket professorial exemption (see *Zahorik v. Cornell University*, 1984).

It could be argued that the institution's treatment of junior nontenured faculty members provides a context for its treatment of the superannuated. The argument would run that the institution is not discriminating on the basis of age, because the young and the old are treated alike; the system that fails to reappoint both the (professionally) young and the old evidences no discrimination. The former argument suffers from too narrow a view of discrimination. It is irrelevant that a sixty-five-year-old is accorded the same status as a thirty-five-year-old; the fact is that the older person has fewer rights at sixty-five than he or she had at fifty-five. If precedent under Title VII is persuasive authority, the total system of an employment policy is no defense against an attack on any one of its elements (*Connecticut v. Teal*, 1982).

*Academic Implications.* The justification for the tenure system is explained in this way: "Tenure is a means to certain ends, specifically (1) freedom of teaching and research and extramural activities and (2) a sufficient degree of economic security to make the profession attractive to men and women of ability. Freedom and economic security, hence tenure, are indispensable to the success of an institution in fulfilling its obligations to its students and to society" (American Association of University Professors, 1984b). Any proposed alternative must withstand scrutiny on both of these accounts.

Ruebhausen does deal with the first element. He argues that a contract, if it is for long enough, will ensure academic freedom. Experience, however, suggests the contrary. No matter how long the institutional commitment is, it is made in anticipation of a later reappointment decision. To that extent, the appointment is one of probation, even if it is of extraordinarily long duration. Thus, it suffers from the same substantive weakness of the periodic or rolling contract, albeit in a more protracted fashion.

Some institutions have provisions to continue employing, on an annual basis, selected faculty members who are beyond the (still temporarily allowed) mandatory retirement age. It could be argued that a contract by which tenure expired in twenty or twenty-five years and the incumbent became eligible for periodic reemployment would function no differently from these existing systems. But existing systems were predicated as a limited exception to a policy of a reasonably late but firm date of retirement. A major change is worked by making such a decision a routine element of the system. It suffices to say that such systems have not been seen as free of threat to academic freedom (American Association of University Professors, 1984a).

Ruebhausen gives scant attention to the second element: the need for institutions to attract able scholars with the promise of security, and the concomitant need to stimulate academic work that may require long periods of gestation. On the contrary, he argues that the long-term contract provides a benefit for institutions that is not supplied by tenure—flexibility. Under the current tenure system, the institution's commitment to the individual cannot be terminated merely out of a desire to reallocate resources. Under Ruebhausen's proposal, however, at the expiration of the term an institution could choose to reallocate the faculty member's position to some other purpose or, for that matter, to use the individual's former salary as institutional savings. A decision so predicated would be insulated from challenge on age-discrimination grounds.

This flexibility, however, would be purchased at the expense of individual security. Accordingly, one must wonder about who would be attracted to the profession when the employment system is expressly geared to eject those who have contributed twenty-five to thirty years of service—a class of faculty members in their late fifties and early sixties—because someone "better" in another discipline is desired, because institutional savings could be realized, because enrollment has surged in other departments, or because of some other "reasonable" factor other than age.

The problems of such a system have been called "massive" (Moore, 1980). Those who are displaced would face critical problems of readjustment. Society at large would have to confront the problem of dealing with a class of displaced senior faculty members. Institutions would also face a dilemma. If pension policies are premised on reasonably late retirement, and if the contribution levels of such plans are so adjusted, then the displaced class would find itself with a relatively meager annuity income and scant professional opportunities elsewhere in higher education. If, however, the contribution policy is premised on the need to maintain substantial income for those who are displaced in their late fifties and early sixties, and if it assumes that a large number in that age group will be discontinued, then the cost of those who will be continued would rise significantly. This would place added economic pressure on the institution to displace more costly senior faculty members and would render the policy or the manner of its administration more suspect under the ADEA (and, in the private sector, under the Employee Retirement Income Security Act as well).

### Conclusion

All the proposed alternatives to the current tenure system, including long-term contracts, have significant problems of administration, of application consistent with federal antidiscrimination laws, and of the degree to which they threaten rather than ensure conditions for the exercise of academic freedom. They present the question of whether the likely impact of abolishing mandatory retirement—a modest rise in institutional costs, and the continuance in service of a small group of faculty members whom the institution might wish to terminate but for whom no good cause for discharge is presented—would justify the serious consideration of any alternative.

If uncapping does present significant institutional problems—a matter by no means certain (Mooney, 1987)—the academic community would be better advised to explore voluntary early-retirement programs and pension policies. One might ask, for example, whether annuity systems that encourage longer service continue to make sense in the absence of firm retirement dates. Alternatively, one should consider whether plans under which faculty members do not fare markedly better by retiring later ought to be explored (see Chapter Five, this volume). In advance of such exploration, and in the absence of any experience under an uncapped ADEA, the abandonment of tenure would be, to put it mildly, a dangerous overreaction.

## References

*Alexander* v. *Garner-Denver Co.,* 415 U.S. 36, 51, 94 S. Ct. 1011 (1974).
American Association of University Professors. "On Periodic Evaluation of Tenured Faculty." *Academe,* 1983, *69* (6), 1a–14a.
American Association of University Professors. *Excerpts from Report on Retirement and Academic Freedom (1968).* Washington, D.C.: American Association of University Professors, 1984a. (Originally published 1968.)
American Association of University Professors. *1940 Statement of Principles on Academic Freedom and Tenure.* Washington, D.C.: American Association of University Professors, 1984b. (Originally published 1940.)
Cartter, A. M. "The Academic Labor Market." In M. Gordon (ed.), *Higher Education and the Labor Market.* New York: McGraw-Hill, 1974.
Chait, R. P., and Ford, A. T. *Beyond Traditional Tenure: A Guide to Sound Policies and Practices.* San Francisco: Jossey-Bass, 1982.
*Connecticut* v. *Teal,* 457 U.S. 440, 102 S. Ct. 2525 (1982).
*Drans* v. *Providence College,* 383 A.2d 1033 (R.I. 1978).
*EEOC* v. *Wyoming,* 460 U.S. 226, 239, 103 S. Ct. 1054, 1062 (1983).
Finkin, M. W. "Regulation by Agreement: The Case of Private Higher Education." *Iowa Law Revue,* 1980, *65* (5), 1119-1146.
Finkin, M. "Commentary: Tenure After an Uncapped ADEA: A Different View." *Journal of College and University Law,* 1988, *15* (1), 43-61.
Greenough, W. C. *College Retirement and Insurance Plans.* New York: Columbia University Press, 1948.
*Leftwich* v. *Harris-Stowe State College,* 702 F.2d 686, 692 (8th Cir. 1983).
*Lloyd* v. *Murphy,* 25 Cal. 2d 48, 153 P.2d 47 (1944).
Machlup, F. "In Defense of Academic Tenure." In L. Joughin (ed.), *Academic Freedom and Tenure.* Madison: University of Wisconsin Press, 1969.

Metzger, W. P. "Academic Tenure in America: A Historical Essay on Faculty Tenure." In AAUP/AAC Commission on Academic Tenure, *Faculty Tenure: Commission on Academic Tenure.* San Francisco: Jossey Bass, 1973.

Mooney, S. "Expected End of Mandatory Retirement in 1990s Unlikely to Cause Glut of Professors, Study Finds." *Chronicle of Higher Education,* Dec. 16, 1987, p. 1.

Moore, K. "Tenure and Retrenchment Practices in Higher Education—A Technical Report." *Journal of the College and University Personnel Association,* 1980, *31* (1), 1-17.

Perry, S. "Formal Reviews for Tenured Professors: Useful Spur or Orwellian Mistake?" *Chronicle of Higher Education,* 1983, *27,* 25.

Player, M. "Proof of Disparate Treatment Under the Age Discrimination in Employment Act: Variation on a Title VII Theme." *Georgia Law Review,* 1983, *17,* 621-648.

Pritchett, H. "A Comprehensive Plan of Insurance and Annuities for College Teachers." *Carnegie Foundation Bulletin,* 1916, *13* (9), 25-94.

Radner, R., and Kuh, C. *Market Conditions and Tenure in U.S. Higher Education, 1955-1973.* Berkeley, Calif.: Carnegie Council on Policy Studies in Higher Education, 1977.

*Rehor v. Case Western Reserve University,* 43 Ohio St. 2d 224, 331 N.E.2d 416, cert. denied, 423 U.S. 1018, 96 S. Ct. 453 (1975).

*Trans World Airlines v. Thurston,* 469 U.S. 111, 126, 105 S. Ct. 613, 624 (1985).

*United States Trust Co. v. New Jersey,* 431 U.S. 1, 25-26, 97 S. Ct. 1505, 1519 (1977).

Van Alstyne, C., and Coldren, S. *The Costs of Implementing Federally Mandated Social Programs at Colleges and Universities.* Washington, D.C.: American Council on Education, 1976.

Van Alstyne, W. W. "Tenure: A Summary, Explanation, and 'Defense.' " *AAUP Bulletin,* 1971, *57* (3), 328-333.

*Zahorik v. Cornell University,* 729 F.2d 85, 34 FEP Cases 165 (2d Cir. 1984).

*Matthew W. Finkin is professor of law, University of Illinois.*

# Index

## A

AAUP/AAC Commission on Academic Tenure, 86, 95. *See also* American Association of University Professors (AAUP); Association of American Colleges (AAC)
Abrams, M., 17, 30
ADEA. *See* Age Discrimination in Employment Act (ADEA)
ADEA amendments, 9-10, 17, 29, 85-86; courses of action under, 92-94; special rule of, 89-92. *See also* Age Discrimination in Employment Act (ADEA); Mandatory retirement age, uncapping of
AFL/CIO, 29
Age: average expected retirement, 38; normal retirement, 73, 74-75; and retirement planning, 65-66; and work behavior, 66-67
Age Discrimination Act of 1975, 17
Age Discrimination in Employment Act (ADEA), 16, 85-86; changes to, 17-18; and long-term contracts, 107-108; and retirement issues, 1-2; and tenure, 101-102; and termination of faculty, 98-101. *See also* ADEA amendments
*Alexander v. Garner-Denver Co.*, 101, 110
Altman, J., 18, 30
American Association of Retired Persons (AARP), 17, 19, 24, 27, 28
American Association of University Professors (AAUP), 2, 5, 21, 23, 24, 28, 30, 34, 49, 74, 75, 78, 83, 98, 106, 108, 110; and higher education lobbying, 20-21
American Council on Education (ACE), 20, 28
American Federation of Teachers (AFT), 29
Anderson, K. H., 64, 71
Appointment without term, 87-88
Association of American Colleges (AAC), 2, 20, 34, 74
Association of American Universities (AAU), and lobbying by higher education, 20, 21

## B

Bartlett, T. A., 20, 21
Beard, E., 23
Bernheim, B. D., 66, 71
Blackburn, J. O., 54, 55, 56, 61
Bona fide occupational qualification (BFOQ), 25-26
Briggs, J., 60
Burkhauser, R. C., 4, 38, 63, 64, 68, 69, 71, 77, 79

## C

Carnegie Foundation, 103-104
Cartter, A. M., 106, 108, 110
Chafee amendment, 21-23
Chafee, J., 21-23
Chait, R. P., 104, 105, 110
Chamber of Commerce, lobbying by, 26, 27
Cherry, H., 80, 83
Civil Rights Act. *See* Title VII
Cohen, W., 17
Coldren, S., 98, 111
*Connecticut v. Teal*, 108, 110
Consolidated Omnibus Budget Reconciliation Act (COBRA) of 1985 (P.L. 99-272), 9, 10
Consortium on the Financing of Higher Education (COFHE), 3-4, 48, 75-76, 83; results of studies by, 51-61
Contracts: long-term, 106-109; short-term, 104-105; tenure, 92-94
Cook, T. J., 34, 49, 77, 83
Corwin, T. W., 48, 49
Cranston, A., 22

113

## D

Defined-benefit plans, 11, 77, 81-82. *See also* Pension plans
Defined-contribution plans, 11, 39, 77, 82. *See also* Pension plans
Donovan, R., 23-24
*Drans v. Providence College*, 106, 110

## E

Early retirement, 73-74
Early-retirement incentive programs (ERIs), 46, 48, 49; and projected retirement dates, 55, 57-59
*EEOC v. Wyoming*, 103, 110
Employee Benefit Research Institute, 11, 13
Employment: long-term contracts for, 106-109; posttenure, 90, 93; short-term contracts for, 104-105
Evaluation, of tenured faculty, 105-106

## F

Faculty: hiring of, 52-54; and inflation and financial incentives, 55-59; MRA programs of, 36-37; response of, to MRA policies, 37-42; termination of, 98-101; voluntary retirement of, 54-55
Faculty buyout plans, 71
Faculty, tenured: evaluation of, 105-106; and MRA uncapping, 1; posttenure employment of, 90, 93; special rule for, 89-90, 91-92
Fields, G. S., 68, 71
Finkin, M. W., 4, 97, 101, 111
Ford, A. T., 104, 105, 110
Ford, L. C., 19, 30

## G

Gray Panthers, 24
Greenough, W. C., 34, 49, 104, 110

## H

Hansen, W. L., 3, 4, 5, 33, 38, 40, 49, 66, 73, 80, 83
Hatch, O., 28

Hawkins, A. C., 19
Hayakawa, S. I., 22
Health, and retirement date, 65
Health insurance. *See* Medical benefits
Heinz, J., 24, 27-28, 29
Higher education: actions on tenure in, 92-94; coping with MRA change in, 46-47; cost of MRA change in, 42-46; faculty response to MRA policies in, 37-42; implications of MRA for, 2-3; lobbying by, 20-21, 29-30; MRA policies in, 34-37; and MRA uncapping, 1, 4-5; and 1985-86 tax changes, 10; research on changing MRA in, 33-34, 47-49; retirement issues for, 1-2
Holden, K. C., 3, 4, 5, 33, 38, 40, 49, 65, 73, 80, 83

## I

Inflation: and retirement expectations, 57
Institute for Research in Social Behavior (IRSB), 52, 55, 56, 58, 60, 61
Ippolito, R. A., 68, 71

## J

Jaqmin, R. A., 52, 53, 54, 55, 61
Johnson, B., 74, 83
Johnson, L. B., 16, 30
Joint Committee on Academic Retirement and Insurance Plans, 74

## K

King, F. P., 34, 49, 77, 83
Kirkland, L., 25
Knepper, P. R., 48, 49
Kotlikoff, L. J., 68, 71
Kreps, J., 17, 18
Kuh, C., 108, 111

## L

Ladd, E. C., Jr., 48, 49
*Leftwich v. Harris-Stowe State College*, 107, 110
Lipset, S. M., 48, 49
*Lloyd v. Murphy*, 104, 110

Lobbying, and mandatory retirement uncapping, 15-30
Lovell, M., 24

## M

Machlup, F., 98, 110
Mandatory retirement: focus on, 17-18; rules on, and work effort, 68-70
Mandatory retirement age (MRA): coping with change in, 46-47; cost of change in, 42-46; faculty response to policies on, 37-42; higher education policies on, 34-37; and hiring and payroll, 52-54; and pension benefits, 77-79; research on raising, 33-34, 47-49; and tax changes, 9-12; and voluntary retirement, 54-55
Mandatory retirement age, uncapping of: and Chafee amendment, 21-23; and Claude Pepper, 18-19; and focus on mandatory retirement, 17-18; and higher education, 1, 4-5, 20-21, 29-30, 70-71; implications of, 2-3; legislative actions on, 23-29; and 1967 ADEA, 16; and pension plans, 73-74, 83; possible effects of, 59-61; retirement timing with, 75-77, 81; studies on, 3-4; and tenure, 4, 97-98, 109-110; and work effort, 70-71
Martinez amendment, 26
Mead, M., 17
Medical benefits, 9, 10
Medicare, 9
Men, work behavior of aged, 66-67
Metzger, W. P., 103, 111
Mitchell, O. S., 68, 71
Montgomery, S., 3, 51, 61
Mooney, S., 110, 111
Moore, K., 109, 111
Moynihan, D., 22, 28
MRA. *See* Mandatory retirement age (MRA)
Mulanaphy, J. M., 48, 49

## N

National Academy of Sciences, 91, 92, 93, 95
National Association of College and University Business Officers, 2
National Association of Independent Colleges and Universities (NAICU), 20
National Commission on Social Security Reform, 8
National Council on the Aging, 24
National Retired Teachers Association (NRTA), 17
Normal retirement age, 73, 74-75

## O

Old Age and Survivors Insurance, 8
Omnibus Budget Reconciliation Act (OBRA) of 1986 (P.L. 99-509), 9-10

## P

Pell, C., 23
Pension benefits: and mandatory retirement age, 77-79; and postponement of retirement, 79-82
Pension plans: effects of Tax Reform Act on, 10-13; types of, 77. *See also* Defined-benefit plans; Defined-contribution plans
Pension policies: in higher education, 34-35; and net wages, 67-68; and retirement decisions, 67; and work effort, 68-70
Pepper, C., 1, 3, 8, 9, 18-19, 24, 25, 26, 28, 29
Perry, S., 106, 111
Player, M., 100, 111
Posttenure employment, 90, 93
Pratt, H. J., 3, 15, 31
Pritchett, H., 98, 104, 111

## Q

Quinn, J. F., 4, 38, 63, 64, 68, 69, 71, 77, 79

## R

Radner, R., 108, 111
Randall, W., 18
Reagan administration, 7, 8
Reagan, R., 23, 24, 29
*Rehor v. Case Western Reserve University*, 106, 111

Reimers, C., 38, 49
Retirement: actual and planned, 63-66; background for initiatives on, 7-8; early, 73-74; of faculty, 3; and pension rules, 67; postponement of, 79-81; termination of tenure as, 88-89; timing of, 75-77, 81; of U.S. work force, 4
Retirement History Study (RHS), 64, 65, 68
Robinson, B., 17, 30
Ruebhausen, O. M., 4, 85, 95, 97, 101-102, 106, 107, 108, 109

**S**

Schiffman, S., 54, 55, 56, 61
Schuck, P. H., 17, 30
Social security: changes in benefits in, 65; deficit in, 8-9, 18; and work effort, 68-70
Social Security Act: and retirement age, 66
Social Security Amendments of 1983 (P.L. 98-21), 8-9
Southworth, J. R., 52, 53, 54, 55, 61
Special rule: duration of, 91-92; for tenured faculty, 89-90; and unlimited tenure, 90-91
Sumberg, A. D., 2-3, 7, 13

**T**

Tax Reform Act (TRA) of 1986, 10-12
Taxes, changes in, 9-12
Tenure: alternatives to, 102-109; as appointment without term, 87-88; as arrangement, 86; courses of action on, 92-94; duration of, 87; employment after, 90, 93; implications of MRA uncapping for, 4; and MRA practices, 34-35; and MRA uncapping, 97-98, 109-110; as terminable, 101-102; termination of, 88-89; unlimited, 90-91

Tenure contracts, 92-94
TIAA plans, 39, 40, 78, 79, 80, 81, 82; and retirement age, 59-61
TIAA-CREF plans, 40, 48, 77, 78, 81, 82
Title VII, of Civil Rights Act, 99, 100, 107, 108
*Trans World Airlines* v. *Thurston*, 100, 111

**U**

Unions, of public safety officers, 25-26
*United States Trust Co.* v. *New Jersey*, 103, 110
Unlimited tenure, 90-91
U.S. Congress, 22, 30; and MRA, 1; 1985-86 legislation of, 9-12; and Social Security Amendments, 8-9
U.S. Department of Labor, 16, 24, 30, 33, 49
U.S. House of Representatives: Committee on Education and Labor, 24, 30; Select Committee on Aging, 19, 23, 30
U.S. Senate: Committee on Human Resources, 22, 30; Special Committee on Aging, 27, 30

**V**

Van Alstyne, C., 98, 111

**W**

White House Conference on Aging, 16, 17, 31
Williams, H., 19, 22
Wise, D. A., 68, 71
Work behavior, of aged, 66-67

**Z**

*Zahorik* v. *Cornell University*, 101, 108